DINO SAFARI

FUN PLACES FOR ADULTS AND CHILDREN TO LEARN ABOUT DINOSAURS

AN AMERICAN SAFARI GUIDE

R. L. Jones

CUMBERLAND HOUSE
NASHVILLE, TENNESSEE

Published by Cumberland House Publishing, Inc.
431 Harding Industrial Drive, Nashville, TN 37211.

Cover design: Unlikely Suburban Design
Cover Art: Dan Brauner
Interior Design: Lisa Taylor

Library of Congress Cataloging-in-Publication Data

Jones, Ray, 1948–
    Dino safari / R. L. Jones.
        p.   cm. — (An American safari guide)
    ISBN 1-58182-035-6 (pbk. : alk. paper)
    1. Dinosaurs—North America.   2. Dinosaurs—North America
Guidebooks.   3. North America Guidebooks.   I. Title.   II. Series.
QE862.D5J67   1999
567.9'097—dc21   99-34629
                                                                        CIP

1 2 3 4 5 6 7 8 — 03 02 01 00 99 98

CONTENTS

PREFACE

ARE YOU A DINO-HUNTER? Sure you are.

Everybody loves dinosaurs, and it's not very hard to understand why. Dinosaurs are big, they're mysterious, and they combine the fact-filled world of science with the wondrous realm of the imaginary. Studying dinosaurs provides insight into the very meaning of existence and can help us find our own proper place on the great wheel of time.

For young and old alike, dinosaurs make learning an adventure. For children, a healthy fascination with dinosaurs can spark an interest in science and help in the development of good reading skills and research habits. What is more, they provide the raw material for terrific science projects.

For adults, dinosaurs can become a lifelong, consciousness-raising hobby—and a highly rewarding one at that. This book was written for dinosaur hobbyists of all ages, people who might describe themselves as "dino-hunters." Just as big-game hunters used to go on safari in Africa, dino-hunters enjoy taking off on expeditions—or "dino safaris"—to libraries, museums, parks, quarries, and trackways—anywhere they are likely to find fossils or facts related to dinosaurs.

Among the dino-hunter's favorite haunts are world-renowned institutions such as the American Museum of Natural

History in New York City, the Peabody Museum in New Haven, Connecticut, the Carnegie Museum in Pittsburgh, the National Museum of Natural History (Smithsonian) in Washington, D.C., the Field Museum in Chicago, or the California Academy of Sciences in San Francisco. These and other key dino-hunting grounds are included in the chapter on America's Top Twenty-Five Dinosaur Attractions (see page 39). You can build an extremely enjoyable vacation or dino safari around any one of these prime dinosaur destinations. They offer fossils, casts, mounted skeletons, models, dioramas, murals, history, technical information, and videos—everything the dino-hunter needs to build a solid foundation of knowledge about dinosaurs and the science of paleontology. But as you'll see, there are hundreds of other excellent places to hunt for dinosaurs, and you'll want to visit as many of them as possible.

Read on and you'll learn how to get the most out of your dino safaris. The following chapters contain detailed information on more than 250 dinosaur museums, parks, and fossil quarries, as well as 200 or more first-rate dinosaur Web sites. (For additional Web site listings and assistance with dino-hunting on the Internet, see our companion volume *Dinosaurs On-Line,* available from booksellers nationwide or from Cumberland House Publishing at 800-439-BOOK.) There is also advice on keeping a dinosaur journal (see "Keeping a Dino-Journal" on page 14) as well as a handy scoring system for keeping track of your safari progress (see "Adding Up Your Dino-Score" on page 13).

At strategic locations throughout the book, you'll find illustrated descriptions of the dinosaurs you'll most likely encounter while on safari, but these are only a sampling. You'll learn about many others at the museums and Web sites you visit. And who knows? Maybe someday you'll discover a whole new type of dinosaur out in the field (for information on guided field expeditions and volunteer opportunities, see "Digging for Dinosaurs," page 266). But even if you don't dig up a dinosaur of your very own, you are bound to learn a lot and have an amazing amount of fun while on dino safari. So grab your pith helmet, your journal or notebook computer—and a copy of this book—and let's go dino-hunting!

Dinosaurs: Up Close and Personal

Have you ever driven down a road, looked off into the forest, and wondered what mysterious creatures might be lurking behind the curtain of trees? Dinosaurs, maybe! If you could see back in there far enough, perhaps you would catch sight of a long-necked *Apatosaurus*, a prickly *Stegosaurus*, a big-horned *Triceratops*, or even a raging *Tyrannosaurus rex* left over from the Mesozoic era. Depending on how long and tiring the drive or how recently you've been to the movies, it is even possible to imagine a dinosaur crashing out of the woods and onto the road right in front of your car. Such things are fun to think about, you say, but they could never really happen, could they? Well, something a little like that *did* happen to me once. Yes, that's right—I had a face-to-face encounter with a dinosaur.

I had flown into the New Orleans airport, rented a car, and headed west along Interstate 10 toward a business appointment in distant Beaumont, Texas. After an hour or so, I pulled over to stretch my legs and give my eyes a break. What they got instead was an *eyeful* of astounding scenery. This was Louisiana's alligator and bayou country, and the rest stop parking area provided an expansive view of one of the world's foremost natural wonders—the magnificent Atchafalaya Basin. Extending out to the horizon was mile after waterlogged mile of growth so primitive-looking and trees so laden with moss and vines that it all seemed to have grown right up out of the remote prehistoric past—let's say, the Jurassic. It seemed that all I needed to do was blink my eyes a few times and I really would see dinosaurs roaming around out there in the Atchafalaya. Maybe there would be a one-hundred-ton *Brachiosaurus* arching its long neck upward to browse through the top limbs of the trees or a hungry *Allosaurus* moving in for the kill on an unsuspecting *Stegosaurus*. Or, if this were the Cretaceous instead of the Jurassic, perhaps I would see a *Struthiomimus*—a personal favorite of mine—clucking through the undergrowth and dining on large insects, a gentle duck-billed *Maiasaura* tending her young, or a deadly *Velociraptor* on the hunt.

Okay, okay, let's face it. I didn't actually see a *Brachiosaurus* or a *Struthiomimus*—I only wished I had seen them. I had come along a little late for that—many millions of years too late. And as a matter of fact, the Atchafalaya Basin, along with much of the rest of Louisiana, was under the ocean during all of the Mesozoic era, also known as the "Age of Dinosaurs." So there were never really any dinos here. There were sea monsters such as ichthyosaurs, plesiosaurs, and mosasaurs—some more than thirty feet long and with jaws big enough to accommodate a Volkswagen. But no dinosaurs, at least not during the Mesozoic. Even so, I was about to meet one, and if you keep reading, so will you.

The experience I had that day in the Atchafalaya produced what I call a *dino-flash*. Often they sneak up on you and strike—like a *Velociraptor*—when you least expect them. You'll be reading *Alley Oop* in the Sunday comics or walking down the street and notice an advertisement for a *Godzilla* sequel and—*wham!*—*dino-flash*! It can happen when you surf the cable television offerings and bump into dinosaurs on five different channels, when you open a magazine and stumble across an article on killer asteroids, when you pick up a stone and realize it's a piece of rock-hard bone, or—yes—even when you're driving through a swamp and pull off the road to stretch your legs. And the reality of it hits you. Dinosaurs were not some cartoonist's fantasy, not some movie-maker's expensive special effect. They were the real thing! They lived right here where we live, on this same small planet. There were little ones, medium-size ones, and big ones—some very big. A few were bigger than anything else that ever walked the earth. There were more different types of them than we will ever know and their hold on the planet lasted perhaps a thousand times longer than our own. When all of that hits you, then there is no doubt about it. You've had a dino-flash.

Of course, you are more likely to have a dino-flash while standing beside a seventy-foot-long skeleton of an *Apatosaurus* in the lobby of a natural history museum. But you can also have one while watching Barney, the purple PBS dinosaur, wave to children from a float in a Christmas parade. It can happen almost anywhere and almost any time. Dinosaur stuff is everywhere nowadays. There are dinosaur novels, dinosaur movies—who has not seen *Jurassic Park*?—dinosaur cartoons and coloring books, dinosaur filling stations and hot-dog stands, even dinosaur mugs (I drink my morning coffee out of one) and bedroom slippers (sorry, but I won't plead guilty to that). It is mind-boggling to reflect on what a tremendous hold these creatures have on the modern mind. This dino-mania is all the more remarkable considering that dinosaurs have been extinct for sixty-five million years—well, most of them have, anyway.

In Dino-land with Alley Oop

My own fascination with dinosaurs began when I was about seven years old. To get me interested in reading the daily newspapers, my dad decided to immerse me in the Sunday morning ritual of perusing the color comics. We sat down together, and the very first strip we read was V. T. Hamlin's delightful *Alley Oop*. In this particular set of panels, the caveman was hungry, so he picked up his trusty club and set off to track down a *Struthiomimus*. I still remember what the unfortunate *Struthiomimus* said—to nobody in particular—just before Oop whacked it over the head. It said "Doo dooly oba."

Keep in mind that *Alley Oop* is all in good fun. It blissfully ignores the fact that the last creature such as *Struthiomimus* passed into oblivion more than sixty million years before the first human being walked the earth. At the age of seven, I didn't know that—and didn't care. I was entranced by the word. My dad helped me to pronounce it: "*Stru-thi-o-mi-mus*." Then I started in with the questions.

"What's a *Struthiomimus*?"

"A kind of dinosaur," he explained.

"What are dinosaurs?" They were not nearly so popular in those days, and strangely enough, I had never heard of them.

"Big lizards," he said. "Great big lizards. Some of them as big as houses."

"Real or make-believe?"

"Real," my dad answered. "Or at least they once were. They're extinct. Gone forever. There are no more of them."

The word *real* hit me like a ton of bricks as did the idea that the world was once filled with marvelous creatures unlike any I had ever seen—and some of them as big as houses. I had just had my first dino-flash.

To me the *Struthiomimus* in the strip looked very much like a big bird without feathers. In fact, once Oop began to cook it over his campfire, his *Struthiomimus* was the spitting image of a Thanksgiving turkey. Not very exciting. But I *was* excited by the idea of dinosaurs in general. Later I would pester my parents and teachers endlessly with questions. The school librarian gave me a children's book about dinosaurs, and the curator of the local youth museum gave me a picture of a prickly *Stegosaurus*. I hung it up on the wall of my room. To get me off their backs, my parents took me to see Walt Disney's *Fantasia*. It had a terrific animated sequence on the earth's prehistory with a *Tyrannosaurus rex* and *Triceratops* locked in mortal combat. After seeing *that*, I was permanently hooked.

My dad's attempt to get me interested in the newspapers succeeded. I still read the paper every day along with the comics and, when I can find it, *Alley Oop*. But my dad's well-meaning efforts had another, unintended consequence. He had turned me into a lifelong dino-hunter.

So What Is a Dino-Hunter?

Dino-hunters are the sort of people who simply cannot resist a movie such as *The Lost World*, who prefer a television documentary on paleontology to any sitcom, who speculate endlessly about doomsday asteroids or comets, and for whom an afternoon at the American Museum of Natural History in New York, the Field Museum in Chicago, or the California Academy of Natural Sciences in San Francisco is more exciting than the Super Bowl. In short, dino-hunters are otherwise ordinary people who just happen to be tremendously interested in great big prehistoric lizards. Don't laugh. You are a dino-hunter too. Otherwise you would not be reading this book.

Dino-hunters do not hunt with guns or bows. Our weapons of choice are curiosity and our own open minds. Our happy hunting grounds consist of libraries, museum exhibits, Internet Web sites, road cuts, spillways, riverbanks, mountains, beaches, deserts—just about anywhere we are likely to come across fossils or dinosaur-related information. Our quarry—what we are after—is to increase our knowledge of the earth's natural history and to experience an occasional, thrilling dino-flash.

Dino-hunters are stubbornly individualistic. We want to find out for ourselves. The way we see it, learning, like life itself, should be an adventure. Too much of what we know about the world around us has been ladled out to us by well-meaning educators following some formulaic academic curricula or dished out to us in tiny sound bites by documentary producers whose mission is more to entertain than to inform. Dino-hunters are convinced that it doesn't have to be that way. If we are energetic enough and willing, we can take the process of discovery into our own hands. The earth is an open book, and regular folks like us can read it. To turn the pages, all we need are a healthy measure of curiosity, a museum pass, or on occasion, a pick and a shovel. That's the same equipment dino-hunters have been using for almost two centuries.

Adding Up Your Dino-Score

Some dino-hunters like to keep track of how well they are doing. Discovery and knowledge are their own rewards, and we really don't need a yardstick to measure their value. Even so, keeping a count of things can be fun. Here is a handy way to score your dino-hunting progress:

1. Give yourself **one point** for each new dinosaur you encounter. Any written description or artist's conception you find in a book, on the Internet, or in a museum will do. Just list the dinosaur's Latin name in your journal and give yourself a point—but only one point per type of dinosaur, please. The illustrations and brief descriptions in this book will get you started.

2. Give yourself **two points** for searching out fossil evidence of your dinosaur either in a book or on the Internet.

Keeping a Dino-Journal

You'll learn more and have more fun if you keep a journal of your safari adventures. It might include lists of fossils, skeletons, and models you've seen, personal observations and insights, sketches, clippings, or printed web pages. If you are a student, your dinosaur journal could become the basis of an award-winning science project. Otherwise, it will serve as a fine souvenir and give you a way to share your hobby with others.

A spiral notebook would serve nicely as a journal. So, too, would a bound sketch pad, but don't use a scrapbook or photo album since you can't easily write in them. Probably your best choice would be a loose-leaf notebook since it can be expanded and you can include plastic folders to protect photographs, color web page printouts, and the like.

You may want to organize your journal alphabetically, dedicating at least one page to each type of dinosaur you've encountered. What is its Latin name? What do scientists know about it? Where did you learn about it? Have you seen a fossil display of this kind of dinosaur? How about a model or a mounted skeleton?

Or you might decide to organize your journal by location, dedicating a page or series of pages to each museum, park, or dinosaur dig you've visited. What did you see there? What did you learn? How was the food? Did the visit increase your dino-score (see Adding Up Your Dino-Score on page 13)?

What you are looking for here are *photographs* of fossils and not necessarily the real thing—that comes next. Many books and Web sites feature pictures of actual fossils. When you find a clearly identified fossil photo, make note of it in your journal and give yourself two more points—but do this only once for each type of dinosaur.

As you can see, it is possible to score up to three points for each dinosaur without ever leaving your house, but the next stage will require a little more effort. To run up a really respectable score, you'll have to travel and visit some of the natural history museums, parks, and other attractions listed in this book.

3. Give yourself **three points** for finding an actual fossil or fossil cast in a museum exhibit or park visitors center. Fossils are the raw material of paleontology. With enough fossils in hand—sometimes only a few are necessary—scientists can make reasonably accurate assumptions about what dinosaurs looked like and how they lived. To see the actual fossilized bones of creatures that walked the earth millions of years ago can be both intriguing and inspiring. When you've located a fossil matching a dinosaur listed in your journal, add three more points to your score.

4. Give yourself **four points** for tracking down a mounted skeleton made from real fossils, casts, or both—most of us can't tell the difference. Articulated skeletons are the most dramatic of all dinosaur exhibits. They show how paleontologists piece together the fossil evidence to get a sense of the complete prehistoric animal. By visiting a museum or park offering full-skeleton exhibits, you will add immeasurably to your knowledge of dinosaurs—and run up your dino-score! However, mounted dinosaur skeletons are rare even in large museums such as the Carnegie in Pittsburgh, the Field in Chicago, or the Academy of Sciences in San Francisco, so you will be

able to reach this stage—and score the maximum of ten points—with a limited number of dinosaurs.

5. Truly adventurous dino-hunters may get a chance to score a bonus—and enjoy an experience of a lifetime. Some museums, parks, and organizations offer volunteer opportunities and guided dino-digs (see Digging for Dinosaurs on page 266). Sign up for one of these and you may find yourself in the field helping to excavate and preserve the remains of an *Allosaurus* or some other fantastically old prehistoric creature. Give yourself a bonus of **ten points** for every type of dinosaur you work with in the field.

The scoring works the same for each dinosaur type. Let's say you've gone the full distance with *Allosaurus*, the fierce Jurassic meat-eater. Having read a description of an *Allosaurus* (one point), located a fossil photo (two points), found a real *Allosaurus* fossil in a museum (three points), and seen a mounted *Allosaurus* skeleton in a museum (four points), you've tallied the maximum score of ten points for this particular animal. And by helping dig for *Allosaurus* fossils out west you've tacked on a ten-point bonus. That's a total of twenty.

No matter how determined you may be, you are unlikely to score twenty or even ten points very often for a single type or species. But since many different dinosaurs are known to science and can be found in museums, grand total scores of more than one thousand points can be achieved. In fact, it is possible to visit a dinosaur wonderland such as the American Museum of Natural Science in New York, the Carnegie Museum in Pittsburgh, or, of course, Dinosaur National Monument in Utah-Colorado and leave with several hundred points in your pocket. Try it! The author doesn't like to brag, but his grand total dino-score now stands at 1,173. No doubt, you can do much better.

The First Dino-hunters

Dino-hunting is an old and respected vocation, one followed by professional scientists and inspired amateurs for nearly two hundred years. Among the first dino-hunters were an English country doctor by the name of Gideon Mantell and his wife, Mary. One day, during the early 1820s, Mary Mantell found a number of large, fossilized teeth—some say in a pile of gravel at the side of a road. Trained in the anatomy of animals as well as people—nineteenth-century doctors often doubled as veterinarians—Dr. Mantell could see that his wife had found something quite out of the ordinary. These were not the teeth of, say, a pig, a dog, or some wild forest creature. They were distinctly reptilian, and much too big to have belonged to any lizard Mantell had ever seen. A jaw large enough to have made use of teeth like these must have been really huge. The animal itself might have been as many as forty feet long and weighed several tons. No, this had been no garden-variety lizard.

Perplexed, Mantell showed the teeth to a museum curator who confirmed that they were indeed an important discovery. Mantell's wife had found the remains of a giant extinct reptile. Judging from the shape of the teeth, it had been a plant-eater—an interesting point since most large modern reptiles are carnivorous. In accordance with the traditions of science, Mantell was given the right to name the species. Recognizing a resemblance between the fossil teeth and those of a modern Iguana, Mantell called the animal an *Iguanodon,* meaning "Iguana Tooth." Later he wrote *The Fossils South of the Downs,* a book about its discovery.

Meanwhile, a geologist and minister named William Buckland was sorting through a collection of fossil specimens gathered near Stonesfield to the north of Oxford, England, and came to an astounding conclusion. What he had arrayed before him were the remains of another enormous prehistoric reptile—not an *Iguanodon* since these teeth were very sharp. Obviously, they had belonged to a carnivore—a very big one—likely more than twenty-five feet long! Buckland gave this fearsome creature a very simple Latin name—*Megalosaurus* or "Big Lizard."

Like Mantell, Buckland published his findings, but while they were discussed in elite scientific and literary circles, it would be some years before these discoveries caught the attention of the public. What was needed was a catchword to fire the imagination. In 1841, British Museum anatomist Richard Owen supplied the necessary verbal spark. Speaking to the British Association for the Advancement of Science, he described the *Megalosaurus* and *Iguanodon* as part of an extinct reptilian suborder he called "dinosaurs," or "terrible lizards."

Owen's dinosaurs became an immediate sensation, turning up in parlor conversation, newspapers, and even novels. The notion that fierce reptilian titans had once gone stomping about the English countryside appealed to the sensibilities of the times. Although stodgy in their personal lives, Victorians were quite adventurous when it came to matters of science and learning. Like us, they also had a taste for the mysterious and colossal. So in the early 1850s, when the Crystal Palace Exhibition Center opened in South London's Sydenham Park, Owen gave his fellow Victorians something big to ponder. He and sculptor Waterhouse Hawkins designed and built a small herd of life-size dinosaur replicas for the Crystal Palace grounds. Their models, which can still be seen, bear little resemblance to the dinosaur replicas we see in museums nowadays. They look something like elephants without trunks. Owen's *Iguanodon* was more suggestive of an ill-tempered hog than of a prehistoric reptile, but it was *big*. In fact, Owen had a long table set up inside the *Iguanodon* and threw a dinner party there for twenty of his friends.

The Bone Wars

In the more than a century and half since Owen coined the term "dinosaurs," interest in these fascinating creatures has never waned and at times has reached a fever pitch. Fossil prospectors have torn apart entire hillsides searching for dinosaur remains, often without finding a single bone. But no matter how difficult the search, people have kept right on looking, and each new discovery has generated a fresh wave of excitement. Stellar careers have been built on foundations consisting of little more than a few scraps of rock.

Competition for possession of key fossils and the right to study, describe, and name new species has always been intense and remains so today. In the early days of dino-hunting it grew so fierce that it touched off feuds between rival scientists, destroying friendships, damaging reputations, and ruining sizable family fortunes. The most celebrated of these "bone wars" was the one between Yale professor Othniel Charles Marsh and Edward Drinker Cope, an inspired amateur paleontologist.

Considering that they shared a powerful common interest, the two men might have become fast friends, but it was not to be. When they first met in 1871, Cope proudly showed off his reconstruction of a plesiosaur skeleton found some years earlier in Kansas. Marsh was ungracious enough to point out that Cope had mounted the skull at the wrong end of the animal— on its tail! It is said Cope was never able to forgive Marsh for the embarrassment this encounter had cost him. Before long America's two most prominent dinosaur experts were circling one another like a pair of angry tyrannosaurids (huge meat-eaters such as the *Albertosaurus* and *Tyrannosaurus rex*). They were about to do battle over an extraordinarily rich scientific prize—the earth's entire 4.6 billion year prehistory.

The first shots of an all-out bone war were fired in 1877 after a pair of startling discoveries were made in Colorado. While hiking near Canon City, in the foothills of the Colorado Front Range, schoolteacher O. C. Lucas stumbled across a cache of huge fossilized bones. Lucas sold the fossils to Cope who hired him to keep digging. A few months later Arthur Lakes, also a schoolteacher, made a similar find near Morrison, a few miles west of Denver. Marsh bought the Morrison fossils for $100, practically from under Cope's very nose, and also sent a crew to dig near the Lucas site in Canon City.

Both these Colorado finds had been made in a layer of reddish rock known today, not coincidentally, as the Morrison Formation. Found in Utah, Wyoming, New Mexico, and several other western states, these rocks date back about 140 million years to Jurassic times. Cope and Marsh now had good reason to believe the formation was rich in dinosaur remains, and subsequent finds would prove them right. Over the next two decades, they each sent team after team to probe ruddy Morrison outcroppings all over the West. A wealthy Quaker, Cope financed his own expeditions while Marsh drew on the assistance of his rich uncle, the noted tycoon George Peabody.

In the end, Cope's long struggle to match the more amply supported Marsh bone for bone, dinosaur for dinosaur, cost him his fortune and perhaps, even his life. He died a broken man in 1897. Although Marsh might have appeared the victor, there can be no real winner in such a conflict. Marsh himself passed from the scene only two years after his great nemesis, and without having convinced either the world or himself that he was the better of the two scientists.

Driven by their maniacal and often destructive competition, Cope and Marsh amassed vast collections of fossils. Much of Cope's collection is now housed at the American Museum of Natural History in New York City, while most of Marsh's dinosaur fossils reside at the Peabody Museum on the Yale campus. The gathering and analysis of these tons of fossils had a tremendous impact on paleontology. Between them, Cope and Marsh discovered or described more than 130 dinosaurs. By the time the old bone-warriors died near the end of the nineteenth century, the world of Owen's "terrible lizards" had become a very crowded place. Now it was inhabited, not just with a few overgrown iguanas, but with sauropods, theropods, and ornithischians, rapacious carnivores and docile plant-eaters, scrambling runts and lumbering giants. In fact, it had become obvious to scientists, if not to the public at large, that 160 million years of evolution had produced a practically end-less number of dinosaur types and species. We will never know or name them all, and perhaps that's just as well. It leaves the door wide open for fresh discoveries.

The *Brontosaurus* That Lost Its Head

And its name! Like everyone, paleontologists sometimes make mistakes, occasionally serious ones. In their feverish rush to describe as many dinosaurs as possible, Cope and Marsh were practically certain to make some whoppers—and they did. Not the least of these was Cope's plesiosaur skeleton with its skull on the end of its tail. Marsh also made blunders, some of which influenced our thinking about dinosaurs for decades. Notable among these was Marsh's confused early description of an animal still widely known by an incorrect name—*Brontosaurus*.

The saga of the *Brontosaurus* began in 1877 with the very Morrison, Colorado, fossil discoveries that helped start the great bone war. Having purchased the fossils from schoolteacher Arthur Lake, Marsh described them as the remains of a long-necked plant-eater he named *Apatosaurus* ("Deceptive Lizard"). Two years later, Marsh received a shipment of bones from a

Wyoming expedition he helped organize and finance. Marsh believed these fossils had belonged to a jumbo-size creature he called *Brontosaurus* ("Thunder Lizard"). Many years later paleontologists would realize that the two animals were one and the same. The *Brontosaurus* was an *Apatosaurus* and visa versa. Since the name *Apatosaurus* came first, scientific tradition made that the proper designation, but even so, the more interesting and popular term "*Brontosaurus*" has persisted down to this day.

Marsh made a far more serious error in 1883 when he set about reconstructing the skeleton of his *Brontosaurus*. Some of the fossils he used were not those of a *Brontosaurus/Apatosaurus* at all, but rather, belonged to a similarly built but otherwise quite different Jurassic plant-eater known as a *Camarasaurus*. Even the skull he mounted on the skeleton was that of a *Camarasaurus*. At least he put it at the correct end of the beast!

One might think paleontologists would recognize this for the scientific blooper it was and quickly set things straight, but that is not what happened. Since the skulls of these animals are rarely, if ever, found attached to their skeletons, any number of skulls found in the same fossil quarry might have been the right one. Scientists remained uncertain about the shape of an *Apatosaurus* skull right down until 1975, when fresh discoveries shed new light on the matter. Apparently, the *Apatosaurus* had a very small head, like that of a *Diplodocus* and very unlike that of the flat-snouted *Camarasaurus*. Since 1975, museum curators all over the world have found themselves climbing up tall ladders to put new skulls on their beloved *Apatosaurus* skeletons.

Getting It Right—Almost

The above story of the *Brontosaurus* and how it got a new name and a smaller head illustrates the beauty of the scientific method. We must always be prepared to let go of convenient beliefs, no matter how much we may cherish them—whenever they are proven wrong. Such an attitude leaves those of us who embrace the scientific method free to judge things for ourselves and not accept everything we are told at face value. It also leaves us free to make mistakes—and correct them later when they are shown to be in error.

All science is built on a foundation of theories, not absolutes, and the same is true of the science of paleontology. Since the fossil record is incomplete, our knowledge of prehistory can never be perfect. Each new and exciting fossil discovery alters our view of the past. The picture changes and will keep changing much as life itself has continued to evolve over the eons. Some ideas make sense. Others don't, and eventually they get weeded out.

Building their theories on a solid foundation of stony fossils, paleontologists keep learning more and more. As if piecing together the skeleton of a massive Jurassic plant-eater, one rib or vertebra at a time, they try to reconstruct the 160 million years of prehistory popularly known as the Age of Dinosaurs. Occasionally, when fresh information shows them to have been wrong about something, they may have to climb up and fit a new head on the beast. Slowly but surely, however, the skeleton is coming together to the delight of scientists, the general public, and dino-hunters like us. Here's a little of what two centuries of dino-hunting have taught us.

The Age of Dinosaurs

The earth is about 4.6 billion years old—that is 4,600 million years. Although we cannot truly comprehend such a vast ocean of time, we can attempt to measure it. Geologists and paleontologists have divided the earth's natural history into immense blocks of time called eras and then subdivided these into periods. Our own era is the Cenozoic or "Modern Age," and the era that came before it was the Mesozoic or "Middle Age." The Mesozoic era is subdivided into three periods, the Triassic, beginning about 248 million years ago, the Jurassic, beginning about 213 million years ago, and the Cretaceous, beginning about 143 million years ago.

Dinosaurs appeared late in the Triassic, about 225 million years before the present, which makes them relative newcomers. That may seem an extraordinary thing to say, but consider this: The earth was already well over 4,300 million years old by the time the first dinosaurs walked the earth. The product of billions of years of evolution, dinosaurs were not primitive creatures, as some mistakenly believe. Instead, they were highly developed and specialized. Using their size, strength, agility, and other advantages, dinosaurs quickly gained ascendancy over other animals and soon filled most of the important environmental niches on land. Throughout much of the Mesozoic, they were the largest and fiercest creatures on the planet. Then, at the end of the Cretaceous, about 65 million years ago, they disappeared—for reasons still not fully understood. In all, they dominated the earth for about 160 million years, a period more than a thousand times longer than our own short reign of perhaps 100,000 years or so.

Some early dinosaurs had hips shaped like those of birds, while others had hips shaped like those of lizards. These two basic types would evolve into a nearly endless array of forms and species. The lizard-hipped variety, or saurischians, gave rise to a pair of important subgroups called sauropods and theropods. The sauropods were mostly big-bodied, four-legged plant-eaters such as the *Apatosaurus* and *Diplodocus*. The theropods were mostly two-legged meat-eaters such as the *Allosaurus* and *Tyrannosaurus rex*. The lizard-hipped variety, or ornithischians, were apparently all plant-eaters. Among the many ornithischians now familiar to dino-hunters were the *Stegosaurus*, *Iguanodon*, and *Triceratops*.

Just as mammals have done in our own Cenozoic era, all these types of dinosaurs evolved and continued to evolve in order to meet the changing circumstances they faced in Mesozoic times. What were those circumstances? How did the world change over the 160 million years between the time the first dinosaurs appeared during the Late Triassic and the time they vanished some 65 million years ago? How did the dinosaurs deal with those changes? Why were they so successful over such a long period? What was the crisis that swept them away at the end of the Cretaceous? Science keeps asking broad questions such as these. However, when professional paleontologists enter a fossil quarry or laboratory, they are mostly interested in more narrowly focused and mundane questions such as how a particular bone might have fit together with another one found nearby. Did the two bones even belong to the same animal? What did an *Apatosaurus* eat? How fast did it walk? Was the *Tyrannosaurus* a hunter or a scavenger? What sort of diseases plagued dinosaurs? Did they get tooth decay?

Asking Questions About Dinosaurs

A big part of the fun of being a dino-hunter is asking questions and trying to solve mysteries—to your own satisfaction, at least. Here are a few examples of the types of questions you might ask and the sort of information you'll be seeking when you visit the museums, parks, and Web sites listed in this book.

What exactly were the dinosaurs?

Although they were related to reptiles, dinosaurs were not just big lizards. The dinosaur skeletal structure was distinct from that of reptiles in a number of important ways. The shapes of their hip, knee, and ankle joints enabled them to walk and run with great efficiency and allowed them to take full advantage of their surroundings and food resources.

What was the earth like during the Age of Dinosaurs?

In the past many dinosaur books and murals tended to give the impression that the Mesozoic earth was one big swamp. This was not the case. Generally speaking, the climate was milder and less variable than today, but there were deserts, mountains, plateaus, plains, rivers, beaches, lakes, and oceans just as there are now.

Early in the Mesozoic era, all the earth's large land masses were clumped together into a single supercontinent called Pangaea. By the beginning of the Jurassic period, Pangaea had begun to break apart, and narrow seaways opened between North America and Europe as well as Africa and Asia. Later Africa, South America, and Antarctica also separated, and all the continents continued to drift apart throughout the Cretaceous.

How many different types of dinosaurs were there?

Dinosaurs were extremely diverse. We are aware of probably only a tiny percentage of the many, many types and species that existed during the 160 million years that land dinosaurs dominated the earth. Since the fossil record is so spotty and difficult to read accurately, we will never know the exact answer to this question, but whatever the number, it is certainly huge.

What did dinosaurs eat?

Paleontologists have studied fossilized stomach contents and droppings—dino-poop—to get a better idea of what dinosaurs ate. Some plant-eaters relished things that we would find very unappetizing today. Sauropods, such as the *Apatosaurus*, apparently had a taste for the foliage of conifers—in other words, pine needles. It has been suggested that the long neck of the *Apatosaurus* gave it a giraffelike ability to reach the more plentiful and tender growth high up in the trees. However, some paleontologists now think the lengthy necks of sauropods served as a sort of vacuum cleaner hose, allowing the animal to eat everything available in a wide area without moving its ponderous body. Of course, meat-eating dinosaurs such as the *T-rex* ate other animals, and in many cases, other dinosaurs. Some may even have eaten their own young.

Were dinosaurs cold-blooded or warm-blooded?

Lizards and other cold-blooded creatures rely on the sun to warm their bodies, while mammals and birds have their own built-in mechanisms for maintaining an optimum body temperature. It was long believed that dinosaurs were cold-blooded like modern reptiles. Now many scientists think otherwise and point to factors such as internal bone structure, the likely high activity levels and metabolic rates of some dinosaurs, and predator-to-prey ratios as evidence. However, the idea that dinosaurs were warm-blooded like modern birds remains controversial.

Other questions might include: *Why were some dinosaurs so large? Were dinosaurs drab like many reptiles today or colorful like modern birds? How long did it take for them to grow to full size? Did they travel in herds? Did carnivorous dinosaurs hunt in packs like wolves? Did dinosaurs roar? Did they call out to warn one another of approaching danger? How did dinosaurs reproduce? Did they care for their young?* The list could go on and on. No doubt, for every question mentioned above, you can add a dozen or so of your own, depending on what happens to interest you.

*A*MONG THE *best-known dinosaurs is the* Triceratops *("Three-horned Face"). With their long horns, massive beaks, and dramatic neck frill armor,* Triceratops *skulls make thrilling museum displays. Luckily for museum curators, large caches of* Triceratops *skulls and other fossils have been found at certain locations in the West. Based on these finds, paleontologists suggest that* Triceratops *migrated across the plains in enormous herds much the way the American bison did before being hunted nearly to extinction during the nineteenth century.*

The Triceratops *is linked in the minds of many museum-goers, if not of all paleontologists, with the even more famous* Tyrannosaurus rex. *Some believe that the* T-rex *preyed on these huge, twelve thousand-pound plant-eaters, perhaps following the massive herds and culling*

TRICERATOPS

out their young, sick, or dying members. With its formidable horns and armor, a healthy adult Triceratops *would have been a very hard kill even for a forty-foot-long* T-rex.

Another similarly horned and armored plant-eater was the Torosaurus *("Bull Lizard"). Weighing up to nine tons and with an armored skull more than eight feet long, it was even better protected than the* Triceratops. *However, it is not so well represented in the fossil record. Mostly it is known through skulls found at a handful of locations in the West.*

Incidentally, both a Triceratops *and a* T-rex *play key roles in the blockbuster novel and movie* Jurassic Park. *However, neither of these were Jurassic dinosaurs. They lived during the Late Cretaceous and apparently continued their deadly dance of predator and prey right down to the end of the Age of Dinosaurs. Perhaps they witnessed the so-called extinction event that wiped out nearly all Cretaceous species.*

There is, of course, one question that interests just about everybody. *What happened to the dinosaurs?*

The Doomsday Asteroid

On that day during the 1820s when Gideon Mantell first laid eyes on the Iguanodon teeth his wife, Mary, had found, the good country doctor must have sucked in his breath in amazement. A trained anatomist, Dr. Mantell would have recognized instantly that these very large, reptilian teeth were unlike those of any animal he had ever studied. It seemed likely they had belonged to some enormous—but long extinct—reptile. Other early dino-hunters would reach similar conclusions regarding their own fossil discoveries. Surely these had been strange and wondrous creatures, but just as surely they were now all long gone. So what happened to them?

This question has been bandied about by paleontologists for the better part of two centuries, and there is still no firm consensus on a likely answer. The longer scientists have studied dinosaurs, the harder they've struggled to account for their disappearance. The *Allosaurus, Apatosaurus, Archaeopteryx, Brachiosaurus, Camptosaurus, Coelophysis, Diplodocus, Herrerasaurus, Iguanodon, Nanotyrannus, Ornithomimus, Protoceratops, Seismosaurus, Stegosaurus, Tenontosaurus, Triceratops, Tyrannosaurus, Velociraptor, Struthiomimus*, and countless other dinosaur types and species have all vanished. But why?

For generations, schoolchildren who asked their teachers about the disappearance of the dinosaurs were given an explanation something like the following: *The world changed but the dinosaurs didn't. As the earth's climate grew cooler, drier, and more variable, the dinosaurs were simply unable to adapt. After all, they were big, slow, stupid, and cold-blooded, unlike the more resourceful mammals—some of which may have had a taste for dinosaur eggs.*

While this answer may satisfy some, any bright ten-year-old can see that it defies common sense. If a changing climate is the answer, why aren't there still dinosaurs around in consistently warm, damp places such as the Amazon Basin, the Congo, or, for that matter, the Atchafalaya? And if mammals were so smart and capable, why didn't they replace the dinosaurs—or eat up all their eggs—a lot sooner? Mammals and dinosaurs shared the earth throughout much of the Mesozoic era. If mammals possessed superior survival skills, they should have won the battle for dominance right from the beginning. They didn't, and we now know at least part of the reason why. The dinosaurs themselves were quite resourceful. They were not *all* so big, so slow, or so stupid and, likely, not cold-blooded either.

Whatever struck down the dinosaurs at the end of the Cretaceous period was an immensely powerful force with comprehensive effects. The fact is, the dinosaurs were only one of many types of creatures that vanished at that time. Reptiles were swept from the sea and the air, and on land every type of creature weighing more than about one hundred pounds became extinct. Some paleontologists cling to the notion that all of this was the work of a gradual but relentless process. Others are convinced that the end came suddenly and dramatically. Of course, you and I are welcome to examine the evidence—the hundreds of museums and Web sites listed in this book provide plenty of information—and decide for ourselves.

While on your dino safari, you are likely to encounter many different versions of the dinosaur extinction story. In some, the villain is an extreme increase in volcanic activity. In others it's continental drift. In still others, it's falling sea levels, the rise of high mountain ranges in Asia and the Americas, or even an exploding star. While each extinction theory has points to recommend it, each also has serious problems. For instance, try as they might, astronomers have found no traces of any nearby

*A*MONG THE *first dinosaurs known to science was the* Iguanodon. *Its discovery and description during the early 1820s by Mary and Gideon Mantell gave rise to the notion that huge and terrible lizards (hence "dinosaurs") had once walked the earth. Nearly two centuries of fossil gathering and analysis have shown this seemingly fanciful idea to be not far from the truth. What creature would more likely inspire terror than a* Tyrannosaurus rex?

Ironically, the Iguanodon *itself was hardly a terrifying animal. An Early Cretaceous plant-eater, its light defensive armament consisted of little more than a short spike on the thumb of its forefeet. On the other hand, at thirty feet in length and weighing up to five tons—about the same as an African elephant—it was certainly huge.*

Although far less formidable than many other dinosaurs, the Iguanodon *must have been highly successful since its fossils can be found in Europe, Asia, Africa, and the American West.*

I G U A N O D O N

32

stars that might have blown up (gone supernova) at the end of the Mesozoic era some sixty-five million years ago.

However, in 1979 a pair of California scientists made a startling discovery, one that caused paleontologists—everyone, really—to look at the sky with renewed wonder. And dread. They found evidence that an asteroid, perhaps as large as six miles wide, had struck the earth sixty-five million years ago at about the time the dinosaurs and countless other creatures disappeared. In many places, Mesozoic (the Age of Dinosaurs) and Cenozoic (after the dinosaurs) rocks are separated by a thin layer of clay. Dr. Walter Alvarez and his father, Luis Alvarez—a Nobel prize–winning astrophysicist—found that this boundary clay is rich in iridium. Although rare on the earth's surface, iridium is relatively abundant in meteors and asteroids. This suggests that, shortly before the clay was deposited, a very large asteroid struck the earth and exploded, flinging iridium-rich particles all around the globe. Such a calamity would have thrown huge clouds of dust into the upper atmosphere, blotting out sunlight for years. Plants would have withered and died along with the animals that depended on them. Temperatures would have dropped, locking everything in ice. Such conditions would have been especially hard on large and highly specialized land animals—in other words, dinosaurs.

From the first, the so-called Asteroid Strike Theory of dinosaur extinction was highly controversial, and it remains so today. Many reasonable objections have been raised and not all of them can be easily explained away. On the other hand, an increasing body of evidence tends to support the asteroid theory. For instance, a large subterranean meteor crater has been found on Mexico's Yucatan Peninsula. More than 180 miles wide and approximately sixty-five million years old, it could be the place where the Age of Dinosaurs came to an end in a single brilliant flash.

SEVERAL TYPES of ostrichlike theropods lived in the Late Cretaceous and perished along with the other dinosaurs at the end of that era. Among these was the Struthiomimus, *a fleet-footed creature very much like modern ground birds except that it lacked feathers. It likely used its stout tail for balance while running. Having no teeth, the* Struthiomimus *was probably a browsing herbivore living off tender shoots and buds. Some believe it may have eaten insects or even eggs stolen from the nests of other dinosaurs.*

STRUTHIOMIMUS

Did the death of the dinosaurs fall from the sky? Might not a similar fate be in store for us someday? These are questions you may want to answer for yourself. Hopefully, this book will help you uncover some vital clues.

Dinosaur on a Tree Limb

You can gather one important clue just by walking outside and looking up in a tree. It is now widely believed that, asteroid or no asteroid, at last one important type of dinosaur survived the mass extinctions at the end of the Cretaceous—birds. Yes, that's right, birds. While it may be hard to accept, a sparrow has a great deal more in common with a *Tyrannosaurus rex* than it does with, say, a mouse or a squirrel. Birds are thought to be close cousins of the theropod dinosaurs, the group that included the *T-rex*, *Velociraptor*, and countless other fierce Mesozoic meat-eaters. Apparently, the birds and theropods descended from a common ancestor that lived sometime during the Triassic.

You may remember that I said I met a dinosaur in the Atchafalaya Basin—and so I did. I also promised to tell you about that—and so, now, I will. That morning, while gazing out into the Louisiana wetlands, I heard a rustle in a nearby tree. I turned my head, and there on a limb was a huge black crow with piercing eyes. I looked at the crow, and a dinosaur looked back.

Dino-Flash!

During the years since, I've given a lot of thought to that experience in the Atchafalaya and wondered what it meant, if anything. Of course it was a personal, highly subjective encounter with no real relevance to science. However, it may have had a little something to offer in the way of understanding. It is the job of professional scientists to collect facts and construct theories to explain them. It is our place, on the other hand, to decide what it all means. So, whenever I am reminded of that crow in Louisiana, it occurs to me that all the earth's creatures are family—all of us partners as well as competitors in the ages-old struggle for survival. Mammals and dinosaurs have shared this planet for more than two hundred million years. Somehow that crow's distant ancestors—and mine—managed to survive the crisis that gripped the earth sixty-five million

35

*T*HE SUPERHERO *and villain among dinosaurs is the Tyrannosaurus* rex *("Tyrant King Lizard"). Children of all ages—shall we say six to ninety-six?—are thrilled at the site of a* Tyrannosaurus *skull, mounted skeleton, or replica. Although such exhibits are common in natural history museums, they usually consist of casts and rarely contain real fossil material. Fossils of* T-rex *are not nearly so numerous as those of many other dinosaurs including its likely prey, the* Triceratops. *In fact, only a few* T-rex *skeletons have ever been located. Their rarity, combined with their popularity, makes them among the most sought after of all fossil remains. Whenever a new* T-rex *find is made, private collectors, museums, and government agencies are likely to fight over it with nearly as much ferocity as the huge carnivores themselves might have done over a fallen* Triceratops.

It is easy to see why people are impressed by the T-rex. *Some forty feet in length and weighing up to* sixteen thousand pounds, it was a heavyweight among land predators. Some paleontologists have suggested that this great beast was not a hunter at all, but rather a carrion-eater. One look at the gaping jaws of its four-foot-long skull is enough to convince most of us otherwise. Indeed, what a frightful hunter this must have been! With its seven-inch-long serrated teeth it could bite off one thousand pounds of meat at a time. Our own puny one- to two-hundred-pound bodies would hardly have served as a snack for this hungry beast.

The Tyrannosaurus lived during the Late Cretaceous in what is now the western United States. At least that is where its fossils have been found. Fossils of a similar animal, the Albertosaurus, have been found in Canada as have those of an equally impressive carnivore, the Daspletosaurus.

REX

years ago and brought extinction to most of their neighbors. Perhaps we humans, the other mammals, and our friends the modern dinosaurs will have what it takes to survive the next crisis, whenever it strikes and in whatever form it may take.

The nonfeathered dinosaurs did not survive the end of the Cretaceous period, but even today their spirits remain with us. Do they ever! Dinosaurs are tremendously popular nowadays, and not just because they've become movie stars. As we have seen, these mostly prehistoric creatures have captivated scientists and the public for more than two centuries. That may be in part because they link the world of hard fact with the world of the imagination. Perhaps it is also because they put us in touch with the true nature of existence by reminding us that we are swimming in a measureless river of time—and we are not alone there.

Enjoy your dino safari!

Top Twenty-Five
North American
Dinosaur Attractions

Academy of Natural Science Museum

Founded in 1812, the Academy of Natural Science Museum in Philadelphia is a world-class institution. Internationally known for its promotion of the sciences, the Academy houses a collection of more than twenty-five million specimens, and it maintains ongoing educational and research programs in dozens of fields. So it should come as no surprise that this museum in the city of Benjamin Franklin—himself a scientist and avid collector—is home to one of the best and most exciting dinosaur attractions in the world.

The Academy poured $4.2 million into its completely renovated and updated Dinosaur Hall, which opened in March 1998. Happily, the designers of this extraordinary prehistory exhibition were able to take advantage of the latest discoveries in paleontology as well as the latest display technology. The hall features an eye-popping array of innovative, multisensory presentations that bring back to life the Age of Dinosaurs. Especially delightful are the animated video displays allowing visitors to actually become a part of the prehistoric landscape. The effect is a bit like seeing yourself on the screen as a character in *Jurassic Park*.

Another remarkable feature of the Academy's new Dinosaur Hall—there are more than a few—is its colossal Mesozoic mural by Philadelphia artist Bob Walters. The mural depicts the entire 160-million-year span (Triassic through Cretaceous) of prehistory dominated by the dinosaurs. It is the first such large-scale dinosaur mural painted since Yale's Peabody Museum unveiled its Rudolph Zallinger masterpiece in the 1940s.

But for all the razzle-dazzle and colorful art, the hall's big models and skeletons are still the Academy's most thrilling and popular exhibits. Hall visitors are welcomed by a pair of grimacing giants—*Tyrannosaurus rex* and the even bigger and more menacing *Giganotosaurus*. An enormous, forty-five-foot-long predator recently discovered in Argentina, the *Giganotosaurus* had a skull more than six feet long and teeth like steak knives—which is more or less what they were. Museum-goers who can slip past these toothy sentinels will find inside the hall an entire herd of mounted skeletons including *Deinonychus*, *Chasmosaurus*, *Hadrosaurus*, *Tenontosaurus*, and many others. Naturally, there are also tons of fossils, some of exceptional scientific and historic importance.

With its mural and outstanding dinosaur exhibition, the Academy of Natural Sciences is a perfect place to begin—or end a dinosaur safari. However, the same can be said for the American Museum of Natural History, the Carnegie Museum of Natural History, the National Museum of Natural History (Smithsonian), and several of the other museums mentioned in this chapter. If you would like a sample before selecting this museum as your starting point, try out the Academy's wonderful Web site (see address below).

Filled with photographs and informative text, it is one of the best dinosaur stops on the Internet.

Academy of Natural Science Museum
1900 Benjamin Franklin Parkway
Philadelphia, PA 19103
(215) 299-1000
www.acnatsci.org/academy.html

American Museum of Natural History

There is probably no better place in the United States to hunt dinosaurs than the American Museum of Natural History. Located on Central Park West in New York City, Teddy Roosevelt's own hometown, this museum of museums is quite a "Bully" institution. Having served science and the public for more than 125 years, it is one of the world's preeminent research centers and is renowned for its vast collections. Only a tiny fraction of its thirty million specimens and artifacts are actually on display. Nonetheless, visitors could spend weeks ranging through the museum's forty halls and galleries without ever seeing anything twice.

The mission of natural history museums in general is to shine the light of scientific reason on billions of years of geological change and evolution. Here at the American Museum that light shines with special brilliance on the Mesozoic era, also known as the "Age of Dinosaurs." No wonder this place is a mecca for dino-hunters.

No wonder, indeed! There may be no more spectacular dinosaur fossil exhibit in America than the one visitors see as they step through the museum entrance into the Theodore Roosevelt Rotunda. There, in a re-creation of a 140-million-year-old drama, a *Barosaurus* mother rears up to a height of nearly five stories to protect her young from a predatory *Allosaurus*. These creatures have been so skillfully mounted that it is possible to forget they are fleshless skeletons.

Beyond the rotunda and its *Barosaurus* is an entire series of prehistory halls, most of them containing mounted dinosaurs or fossil materials. Among the key dinosaur fossils or mounted skeletons you'll see here are those of *Camarasaurus, Diplodocus, Apatosaurus, Coelophysis, Albertosaurus, Struthiomimus, Ornitholestes, Oviraptor, Velociraptor, Camptosaurus, Pachycephalosaurus, Triceratops,* and many others. In all, more than six hundred dinosaur specimens are on display in the six halls devoted to vertebrate evolution. There are also plenty of interactive or multimedia exhibits, time lines, and other interpretive aids to help you build a solid base of knowledge on the subject of dinosaurs.

To start your dinosaur adventure you don't have to go to Manhattan. The museum maintains one of the most colorful and informative Web sites on the Internet. Accessible at the address below, it contains all the information you'll need to plan an enjoyable visit. But travel information is only a small part of what you'll find here. A wide variety of museum-related topics are wonderfully illustrated on the Web site. Particularly attractive are its *Fifty Treasures* pages offering a "virtual tour" of some of the museum's most important and best-known exhibits. Among these are color photographs and articles on the *Barosaurus,* dinosaur embryo, dinosaur mummy, dinosaur track, and *T-rex* displays. Also included—and not to be missed—are pages on the Star of India gem, komodo dragon lizard, equine evolution, Cape York meteorite, Ice Age art, giant Sequoia, blue whale, Tasmanian wolf, passenger pigeon, and mastodon.

American Museum of Natural History
79th Street and Central Park West
New York, NY 10024
(212) 769-5100
www.amnh.org

43

DIPLODOCUS

*W*ITH A *length of almost ninety feet, but weighing in at a* mere *twenty thousand pounds, the* Diplodocus *was slim and trim compared to its fellow Jurassic sauropod, the sixty thousand-pound* Apatosaurus. *The* Diplodocus *was not as stocky as some other sauropods because much of its length was taken up by its neck and tail. The* Diplodocus *("Double Beamed") has lent its name to an entire group of sauropods known as the Diplodocids, one of which was the* Apatosaurus.

Another large Diplodocid was the Barosaurus, *which lived in northern forests during the Late Jurassic. Built much like the* Diplodocus, *it had an even longer neck, allowing it to eat leaves at the very tops of trees. Because of their extraordinary length* Barosaurus *skeletons are quite dramatic when mounted for museum display. The one at the American Museum of Natural History in New York City was assembled using lightweight casts since real fossilized bone would have been much too heavy to be mounted in this way. Fossils of the plant-eating* Barosaurus *are extremely rare but have been found in several western states as well as Africa.*

BAROSAURUS

Carnegie Museum of Natural History

The Carnegie Museum of Natural History is one of several Pittsburgh museums under the wing of the Carnegie Institute, established by steel magnate and philanthropist Andrew Carnegie. Among the others are the Carnegie Museum of Art, Carnegie Science Museum, and Andy Warhol Museum. As a Carnegie brochure puts it, these institutions offer everything "from Jurassic insects to diamonds, Matisse masterpieces to Andy Warhol, towering dinosaurs to a four-story Omnimax theater."

While likely to appreciate all these marvels, committed dino-hunters will have little time for them until the Carnegie's famed Dinosaur Hall has been thoroughly digested—and that takes time. The hall takes visitors on an epic journey through the Triassic, Jurassic, and Cretaceous Periods, providing close encounters with giant sauropods such as *Diplodocus* and *Apatosaurus*, bird-hipped plant-eaters such as *Dryosaurus* and *Camptosaurus*, and fierce meat-eaters such as *Tyrannosaurus rex* and *Allosaurus*.

The Carnegie's fossil collection includes evidence of all but a few of the 370 varieties of dinosaur thus far known to science. For more than a century, this world-famous museum has been an epicenter of dinosaur studies, and it remains so today. In fact, many of the dinosaurs found here were first discovered and described by paleontologists working for the Carnegie Museum. As early as the 1890s, the Carnegie had teams in the field searching for dinosaur fossils. In 1909, a Carnegie-funded expedition discovered the rich Utah fossil quarry now known as Dinosaur National Monument. Many of the fossils you'll see at the Carnegie were excavated there.

Naturally, you'll see much more in the Carnegie's prehistory halls than just dinosaurs—as if they weren't enough. There are icthyosaurs, mosasaurs, pterosaurs, and a host of invertebrates on hand for study. In the Fossil Mammal Hall, which does the same thing for the Cenozoic period that the Dinosaur Hall does for the Mesozoic era, there are mammoths, mastodons, camels, horses, and saber-toothed cats.

The Hall of Geology helps put life on our planet into the nearly infinite perspective of geological time, and you should put it on your schedule. Don't miss the Time Tower, which illuminates 4.6 billion years of earth history with hundreds of tiny lights.

The Carnegie's on-line exhibits are among the best you'll see on the Internet. While offerings change occasionally, there is usually at least one dinosaur exhibit featured on the Carnegie Web site. Other on-line exhibits touch on anthropology, archaeology, geology, and exploration.

> Carnegie Museum of Natural History
> 4400 Forbes Avenue
> Pittsburgh, PA 15213
> (412) 622-3131
> www.clpgh.org/cmnh

Harvard Museum of Natural History/Museum of Comparative Zoology

As one might expect, Harvard is a haunt of dinosaurs. America's most famous university is home to one of the nation's best-known paleontology collections—that of the Museum of Comparative Zoology. The exhibits at this museum do, indeed, suggest some extraordinary comparisons. Here visitors will encounter a forty-two-foot-long *Kronosaurus* (a rather vicious-looking marine reptile) as well as a diminutive pheasant once owned by George Washington, a coelacanth from the Indian Ocean as well as a 1,600-pound amethyst geode from Brazil, an absolutely unique display of glass flowers, as well as an almost endless array of Mesozoic fossils. If the world had an attic, this might be it.

The sort of people who enjoy pawing through dusty old trunks may find this museum endlessly engaging, but so, too, will dino-hunters. The *Triceratops* skeleton here was among the first ever discovered. Also on display are mounted skeletons of *Deinonychus, Allosaurus, Plateosaurus* (an early sauropod-like plant-eater), and several other dinosaurs as well as the flying reptile *Pteranodon* and the sail-backed *Dimetrodon*. You may find the seven-foot-long prehistoric turtle shell almost as impressive as the dinosaur fossils.

The broad scope of this museum is owed in part to its founder, famed zoologist Louis Agassiz, who was born in Switzerland in 1807. Agassiz served as the museum's director from the day it opened its doors in 1859 until his death in 1873. The comparative relationships between species fascinated Agassiz, and he sought to illustrate them in the museum's exhibits.

The Museum of Comparative Zoology is now part of the larger Harvard Museum of Natural History. These museums offer a variety of educational workshops and travel programs, which occasionally focus on dinosaurs or other paleontological subjects. One recent series of family programs was called *Digging for Dinosaurs* and gave parents a chance to explore the dinosaur phenomenon with their children.

Harvard Museum of Natural History/Museum
of Comparative Zoology
26 Oxford Street
Cambridge, MA 02138
(617) 495-3045
www.mcz.harvard.edu
www.hmnh.harvard.edu

*M*UCH SMALLER *than most other Jurassic sauropods, but apparently more widely distributed, was the twenty-ton* Camarasaurus. *The first* Camarasaurus *skeleton was discovered during the 1920s at Dinosaur National Monument in Utah. Later, its fossils turned up in several other western states. Like other sauropods, it may have traveled in herds, migrating in search of better grazing. The juvenile* Camarasaurus *on display at the Carnegie Museum in Pittsburgh is said to be the most complete sauropod skeleton ever found.*

CAMARASAURUS

National Museum of Natural History
(Smithsonian Institution)

Forget the power and the politics. Washington, D.C., is a kid's place. Just ask any eleven-year-old who has visited our nation's capital on a school field trip or a family holiday outing. With its government buildings, marble monuments, reflecting pools, museums, street vendors, and National Zoo, Washington is more fun than any amusement park, and the best part about it is that everything here is real, not make-believe. Among the city's many youth-inspiring wonders are a pair of attractions no kid wants to miss. One is the Air and Space Museum—because that's where they keep the spaceships. The other is the Smithsonian Institution's National Museum of Natural History. Why? Because that's where they keep the dinosaurs!

Dino-hunters young and old know they are at the right place when they catch sight of Uncle Beazley, the bronze *Triceratops* on the Capitol Mall not far from the museum entrance. But the best stuff is *inside* the museum. Many American youngsters as well as adults get their first look at real dinosaur fossils at the Smithsonian, and it is quite an eye-full. An entire hall on the main floor is devoted to dinosaur dioramas, skeletons, skulls, and other fossil materials. There are so many fossil mounts here that you may feel you are standing in the midst of a whole herd of dinosaurs. However, since the skeletons date from three different periods of the 183-million-year Mesozoic era, no herd like this one ever existed—at least not in the flesh.

Among the highlights of the Dinosaur Hall are an eighty-seven-foot-long *Diplodocus longus*, a grimacing *Allosaurus*, threatening even as a skeleton, and a full-sized *Stegosaurus* with bony back plates and spiked tail. You'll also see *Albertosaurus, Brachyceratops, Triceratops, Camarasaurus, Camp-*

50

tosaurus, Ceratosaurus, Edmontosaurus, Maiasaura, Tyrannosaurus rex, and countless other mounted skeletons, models, skulls, tracks, casts, and fossils. There are flying reptiles such as *Quetzalcoatlus, Pteranodon,* and *Rhamphorhynchus* as well as giant marine reptiles such as the icthyosaur, mosasaur, and plesiosaur. Illustrative dioramas place some of these creatures in the habitats scientists believe were typical of their respective periods.

Of course, the reach of this museum extends far beyond the Mesozoic. For instance, visitors will find an abundance of Cenozoic exhibits including rare early mammals and Ice Age giants such as the mammoth and mastodon—few museum-goers can forget the titanic elephant on display at the entrance. In fact, there are informative exhibits on every era of prehistory and practically every aspect of paleontology. The National Museum provides a solid grounding in the principles of paleontology as a science and in the development of dinosaurs as a species.

It would be a shame to visit the Smithsonian without taking the time to visit a few of its other halls, museums, and galleries. Even the most dedicated and single-minded dino-hunter is likely to feel the magnetic pull of their many attractions, so leave plenty of time to enjoy them. Of course, you won't be able to see everything. It has been said that it would take an entire lifetime to do justice to every exhibit at the Smithsonian.

> National Museum of Natural History
> (Smithsonian Institution)
> Washington, DC 20560
> (202) 357-1300
> (202) 357-2020 (for recorded travel information)
> **www.nmnh.si.edu**

*A*LTHOUGH VERY *much smaller than carnosaurs such as the* Albertosaurus *and* Tyrannosaurus rex, *the seven-foot-long* Velociraptor *("Swift Robber") was nonetheless a formidable predator. Its brain was large relative to its size—something that could not be said for most dinosaurs—and it could easily outmaneuver its prey. An important part of its arsenal was a razor-sharp sickle attached to its strong hind limbs. No doubt, it could gut an enemy with a few swift kicks. Hunting alone or in packs, it could bring down prey many times its own size. The Late Cretaceous* Velociraptor *has been found in Asia.*

VELOCIRAPTOR

Somewhat similar to the Velociraptor *was the* Deinonychus *("Terrible Claw"), which lived much earlier in the Cretaceous period. With a length of about 12 feet and weighing up to 150 pounds it was a highly capable hunter. With lightweight bones, much like those of birds, it was built for speed rather than strength, but its hooked and bladed claws could quickly shred the flesh of an enemy. Found in the northern Rockies,* Deinonychus *fossils are seen in many museum collections including the one at the Peabody in New Haven.*

D
E
I
N
O
N
Y
C
H
U
S

Peabody Museum of Natural History

Yale's renowned Peabody Museum of Natural History in New Haven, Connecticut, is an institution created by and for dinosaurs. The museum was established in 1866 with an endowment provided by banking tycoon George Peabody, the uncle and benefactor of bone-warrior O. C. Marsh. A Yale professor and noted paleontologist, Marsh was among the first to be led by his own raging curiosity along the path of inquiry we are now following—he was a dino-hunter. It was here at the Peabody Museum that Marsh built and stored his vast collection of dinosaur fossils. The Peabody still houses many of the fossils he and his teams of devoted Yale students discovered more than a century ago.

Not surprisingly, the Peabody's most widely celebrated exhibition is its Great Hall of the Dinosaurs. Hall visitors are greeted by a seventy-foot-long *Apatosaurus* skeleton excavated by Marsh himself during the 1870s. Inside the hall they'll see examples of *Stegosaurus, Triceratops, Deinonychus, Velociraptor, Centrosaurus, Anatosaurus, Chasmosaurus, Torosaurus, Archaeopteryx* (the first fossil to show a transitional relationship between dinosaurs and birds), and of course, the king of dinosaurs and dino-exhibits, *Tyrannosaurus rex*. There are fossils, casts, mounted skeletons, and models of these and many other inhabitants of our planet's crowded past.

However, the Peabody's most impressive and famous display is not a skeleton, but rather, a painting. Overlooking the Great Hall is Rudolph Zallinger's massive, 110-foot-long mural depicting three hundred million years of earth history from Devonian times right down through the Cretaceous. Known as the *Age of Reptiles*, the sixteen-foot-high mural took four-and-a-half years and more than seven thousand hours of work to complete. Zallinger painted the mural during the 1940s, using

54

the best scientific information available at the time. He filled it with plants and animals that museum experts had told him would accurately portray natural history. In effect, Zallinger took a snapshot of what paleontologists thought half a century ago. Of course, science has marched on, and some of the notions that influenced Zallinger's mural have been left far behind. What remains fresh, however, is the mural's ability to recall the dark past and bring it to life again in the bright realm of our imaginations.

Committed dino-hunters will be so captivated by the Peabody's dinosaur offerings that they may not find time to enjoy some of its other fabulous exhibits. They should try, somehow, to make the time. There are meteorites on the second floor as well as a Discovery Room sure to fascinate children. Elsewhere in the museum are rare rocks, minerals, gems, modern bird displays, and anthropology exhibits on Native American, Pacific, and South American cultures.

> Peabody Museum of Natural History
> Yale University
> 170 Whitney Avenue
> New Haven, CT 06520
> (203) 432-5050
> www.peabody.yale.edu

MIDWEST

Field Museum of Natural History

Chicago's Field Museum was created in 1893 to serve as an attraction of the famed Colombian exposition. It was the "Gay Nineties" and fair visitors lined up for miles to ride the world's first Ferris wheel, but they also descended in droves on the Field. Most of them had never seen anything to match the

BRACHIOSAURUS

*W*ITH ITS *long forelimbs and very long neck enabling it to browse high in trees, the* Brachiosaurus *was the giraffe of the Late Jurassic. It was more than a little bit larger than a modern giraffe, however—larger, in fact, than almost anything else that ever walked the earth. Some think this 90-foot-long sauropod may have weighed up to 110 tons, or about 220,000 pounds. Had they lived at the same time, instead of being separated by about 140 million years of natural history, a* Brachiosaurus *might have stepped on a 1,000-pound giraffe and hardly even noticed it was there.*

Interestingly, the Brachiosaurus *had nostrils on top of its head. This adaptation once led some paleontologists to think the animal might have walked along underwater, using its long neck like a snorkel, but analysis has shown that its lungs could not have withstood the water pressure.* Brachiosaurus *fossils have been found mostly in Colorado and Africa.*

museum's massive assortment of natural history specimens. Among these were dinosaur fossils, and no doubt they drew plenty of attention—dinos were a hot museum attraction then, just as they are today.

Now more than a century old, the Field continues to fascinate visitors with dinosaur fossils, casts, mounted skeletons, and models. *Albertosaurus*, *Apatosaurus* (once known as *Brontosaurus*), and *Brachiosaurus* are among the standouts in Dinosaur Hall, which was remodeled as part of the museum's centennial in 1994. Cenozoic exhibits include excellent examples of mammoth, mastodon, saber-toothed cat, and other mega-mammals.

The museum's paleontology exhibits are intended not just to thrill, but to transport the visitor through the 3.8-billion-year history of life on the earth. Exhibits are updated frequently to keep them abreast of the latest scientific discoveries. An on-site fossil laboratory allows visitors to watch museum staff and volunteers prepare bones for study and display. Like the American Natural History Museum in New York, the California Academy of Sciences in San Francisco, the National Museum of Natural History in Washington, D.C., and a few other such institutions around the country, the Field provides an excellent overview of paleontology in general and the study of dinosaurs in particular.

A toothy *Tyrannosaurus rex* with the unlikely name of Sue may soon become the museum's biggest dino-attraction. The most complete dinosaur skeleton ever collected, Sue was uncovered near the little town of Faith, South Dakota, in 1990 and very soon became the object of a tug of war between several prospective owners and the U.S. government. The in-and-out-of-court squabble ended only after the Field stepped in and bought the skeleton. Sue will be placed on display at the museum in 2000. Approximately 90 percent—an extraordinarily large portion—of Sue's fossilized bones were recovered, and this is allowing scientists to study the *T-rex* as never before. Only twenty-two other *T-rex* skeletons have been discovered and none is as complete as Sue. Of special interest to dino-hunters and kids is the "Sue" on-line exhibit. You can access it at the second Web site address listed below.

Field Museum of Natural History
1400 South Lake Shore Drive
Chicago, IL 60605
(312) 922-9410
www.fmnh.org
www.fmnh.org/sue
www.fmnh.org/exhibits/dino/triassic.thm

Milwaukee Museum

The lucky citizens of Milwaukee, Wisconsin, can boast one of the best public museums in America—and one of the oldest. It dates to 1882 when a local natural history society donated some twenty-thousand specimens to the city. The museum built to house this collection contained one of the nation's first total-habitat dioramas—showing a family of muskrats in their natural surroundings. Although quite familiar to museum-goers nowadays, this type of display was considered highly innovative at the time. It became known as the "Milwaukee Style" and can still be seen in museum dioramas around the country.

Innovative exhibits remain a hallmark of the Milwaukee Museum, where high-tech, interactive displays help bring geography, history, science, anthropology, archaeology, geology, and paleontology to life for visitors. With its dinosaur displays, the museum pushes its century-old environmental style well into the twenty-first century. In an exhibition known as

Third Planet, mounted skeletons and models of *Stegosaurus*, *Triceratops*, *Tyrannosaurus*, and many other dinos are shown in what are believed to have been their native habitats.

The Milwaukee Museum's curators have plenty of material to draw on when composing their exhibits. Over the last century, collections have grown from the original twenty thousand specimens and artifacts to well over five million, and more are being added every day. The museum sponsors scientific expeditions throughout the world. One such expedition in 1981 turned up the remains of the *Torosaurus* or "Bull Lizard" skeleton now on display at the entrance to the *Third Planet* exhibition.

Naturally, the museum Web site is also exceptional and includes a wealth of material on dinosaurs, dinosaur extinction, and fossils. The museum's geology department has its own separate Web site. Both sites can be accessed at the address below.

> Milwaukee Museum
> 800 West Wells Street
> Milwaukee, WI 53233
> (414) 278-2702 (recorded information)
> (414) 278-2700 (receptionist)
> **www.mpm.edu**

Saint Louis Science Center/Dinosaur Park

Dinosaurs are, perhaps, the biggest attraction of the Saint Louis Science Center. Everyone who comes here wants to see the dramatic diorama featuring a *Tyrannosaurus* attacking a *Triceratops*, but there is much more to see here. A substantial collection of dinosaur material can be found in the center's *Ecology and Environment Past and Present* exhibition where there are many fossils and life-size robotic models on display.

Another exciting dinosaur exhibit can be found outside in the museum picnic area. Called Dinosaur Park, it is filled with full-size models. Here *T-rex* and other dino-favorites keep children and adults company while they munch on their chicken sandwiches. Those who would prefer to eat their lunch in the shadow of scientific giants rather than prehistoric ones can sit inside at the Einstein Cafe.

The center offers an excellent on-line gallery and tour accessible at the Internet address below. It includes more than 300 separate pages of information and 150 color photographs.

> Saint Louis Science Center Dinosaur Park
> 5050 Oakland Avenue
> Saint Louis, MO 63110
> (314) 289-4400
> www.slsc.org

SOUTH

Fort Worth Museum of Science and History

With more than 100,000 specimens and artifacts available for study and display, the Fort Worth Museum of Science and History has plenty to offer scientists and natural history buffs. But as the fourteen-foot-tall *Acrocanthosaurus* standing guard at the entrance suggests, this museum is especially attractive to dino-hunters. Inside the building, a 2,200-square-foot exhibition illustrates highlights from *Lone Star Dinosaurs*, the well-known book by Southern Methodist University dinosaur expert Dr. Louis Jacob. The exhibition includes fossils, casts, and film footage of dinosaur excavations in various parts of Texas. In addition to the *Acrocanthosaurus* (a Cretaceous meat-eater), featured dinos include *Pleurocoelus* (a seventy-foot-long, twenty-ton plant-eater), *Chasmosaurus, Nodosaurus, Hadrosaurus, and Tyrannosaurus rex.*

Perhaps the museum's most delightful feature is an outdoor area where you can conduct your own excavations. Called *DinoDig*, this unusual hands-on exhibit is a replica of an actual Texas fossil quarry containing casts of real *Tenontosaurus* fossils. To make sure the *DinoDig* experience is true to life and scientifically accurate, museum staff have consulted extensively with Dr. Jacob. There is an added touch of fantasy, however, since full-sized dinosaur models keep watch over amateur paleontologists while they work.

> Fort Worth Museum of Science and History
> 1501 Montgomery Street
> Fort Worth, TX 76107
> (817) 732-1631
> **www.fwmuseum.org**
> **www.fortworth.org/local/museum.htm**

Houston Natural Science Museum

This complex of educational attractions includes a planetarium, observatory, and Imax theater as well as several exhibit halls. Of primary interest to dino-hunters is, of course, the Paleontology Hall with its nine thousand-square-foot "Life Through Time Exhibition." Allow plenty of time for exploring this well-designed and innovative exhibition.

A fifty-foot, backlit mural by William Stout provides an excellent starting point. Many of the creatures shown in the 4,500 million years depicted in the mural turn up in fossil displays elsewhere in the hall. At the heart of the hall is its Mesozoic section where you'll encounter a seventy-eight-foot-long *Diplodocus* skeleton and a twenty-eight-foot real-fossil mount of a duck-billed *Edmontosaurus* as well as a forty-five-foot-long model of *Tyrannosaurus rex*. A thrilling Cretaceous diorama shows a predatory *Dromaeosaurus* leaping from a cliff face in

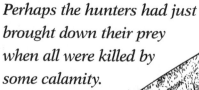

T E N O N T O S A U R U S

A CRETACEOUS SPECIES *common in what is now the southwestern United States, the* Tenontosaurus *was a plant-eater weighing about five tons. While it looked a bit like an* Iguanodon, *the* Tenontosaurus *is thought to have evolved from a group of relatively small dinosaurs called (by those with tongues slippery enough to pronounce the word) hypsilophodontids. Most other members of this herbivorous group were bipedal, but the considerably larger* Tenontosaurus *had four legs. Although its trunk and neck were about twelve feet high, the long tail of the* Tenontosaurus *stretched out some fifteen feet or more. No one is quite sure how this amazing tail served the animal's survival needs, but it may have provided a counterweight for the body when rearing up to bite off hard-to-reach foliage.*

The Tenontosaurus *was likely a frequent target of carnivores such as the pack-hunting* Deinonychus. *A dramatic fossil discovery in Montana yielded a single* Tenontosaurus *skeleton surrounded by several skeletons of the predatory* Deinonychus. *Perhaps the hunters had just brought down their prey when all were killed by some calamity.*

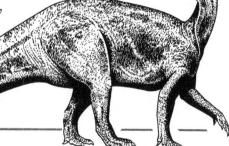

pursuit of an *Ankylosaurus*. The hall also features models, casts, and fossils of *Stegosaurus*, *Quetzalcoatlus*, *Deinonychus*, *Archaeopteryx*, and many other types.

Increasingly, museums throughout the country are replacing their display fossils with less fragile and far less expensive casts. But not so in Houston. Most of the 450 specimens you'll see here are composed of actual fossil materials, although there are a few fiberglass models.

> Houston Natural Science Museum
> One Hermann Circle Drive
> Houston, TX 77030
> (713) 639-4600
> **www.hmns.org**

ROCKY MOUNTAINS AND SOUTHWEST

Denver Museum of Natural History

The Denver Museum of Natural History has long been known for its impressive fossil displays and meticulously crafted dioramas depicting both modern and prehistoric wildlife. In 1995, the museum added to its renown with the opening of one of the nation's finest natural history exhibits. Known as "Prehistoric Journey," it is by far the museum's largest and most ambitious permanent exhibition. Covering some seventeen thousand square feet of floor space, it took more than six years and $7.7 million to create. It includes a working fossil laboratory with a public viewing area.

The exhibition retraces earth's 4.5-billion-year history and tells the story of the appearance and evolution of life on the planet. Naturally, dinosaurs play an important role in this rather all-encompassing story and are pretty much the stars of the show. In addition to the always popular *Tyrannosaurus rex*, there are fully mounted skeletons of *Stegosaurus*, *Diplodocus*, *Coelophysis*, and *Lambeosaurus*. Dino-dioramas help visitors imagine the world these fascinating creatures inhabited.

For those who want to continue the work of unlocking the mysteries of the earth's past, the museum operates a certification program for paleontology lab and fieldwork. The course, taught by museum curators and associates, is open to adults age seventeen and older. Call the museum for schedules and other information on this exciting educational opportunity.

> Denver Museum of Natural History
> 2001 Colorado Boulevard
> Denver, CO 80205
> (800) 925-2250
> (303) 322-7009
> (303) 370-6303 (for courses)
> **www.dmnh.org**

Devil's Canyon Science and Learning Center
Dinosaur Discovery Museum
Dinamation International Society

You may have heard of Dinamation, the robotics firm that builds many of the lifelike models seen in dinosaur movies and museum displays. Dinamation founder Chris Mayes had both science and fun in mind when he launched the southern California firm more than a decade ago. Models built by Dinamation make use of the latest paleontological discoveries and the best animation technology available.

Recently, Dinamation created its own permanent exhibit in Fruita, Colorado, near the heart of Colorado's fossil-rich dinosaur country. The Devil's Canyon Science and Learning Center and Dinosaur Discovery Museum offer interactive videos, a state-of-the-art fossil laboratory, and displays of important fossil discoveries as well as more than a dozen dioramas featuring Dinamation's delightful life-size models. There is even an earthquake simulator on hand to shake up the imagination. Of particular interest to dino-hunters is a program allowing volunteers to dig for dinosaur fossils.

> Devil's Canyon Science and Learning Center
> Dinosaur Discovery Museum
> Dinamation International Society
> 550 Jurassic Court
> Fruita, CO 81521
> (970) 858-7282
> (800) DIG-DINO (for those interested in digging
>   for fossils)
> **www.digdino.org**

Dinosaur National Monument

In 1907, a paleontologist, explorer, and fossil prospector by the name of Earl Douglass came to Utah in search of Early Cenozoic mammal bones. Douglass was successful and sent carloads of forty-million-year-old fossils back east to his employers at the Carnegie Museum in Pittsburgh. By 1909, Douglass had worked his way into the Uinta Mountains in the northeastern corner of the state near the Colorado border. What he found there would astonish him and the entire scientific world.

Exposed along the flanks of the Uintas is a thick layer of reddish rock known as the Morrison formation. The Morrison began about 150 million years ago as an enormous floodplain, which at one time or another would stretch across parts of Utah, Colorado, Wyoming, Montana, South Dakota, New Mexico, and Oklahoma. Over many millions of years, sediments were laid down burying the carcasses of dead

W ITH ITS *menacing jaws, daggerlike teeth, sharp talons, and powerful legs, the* Allosaurus *surely ranks among the fiercest creatures ever to walk the earth. A Late Jurassic meateater, it grew to thirty-five feet or more in length and weighed up to one and a half tons. Although some paleontologists believe it may have been a scavenger, the* Allosaurus *likely preyed on large plant-eaters such as the seventy-foot-long sauropod* Apatosaurus. *Allosaurs may have hunted in packs to bring down the much larger sauropods. Once it had made a kill, an* Allosaurus *could bite off huge chunks of meat with its serrated teeth, which have been compared to long knives.*

ALLOSAURUS

In part because it resembles the wildly popular Tyrannosaurus rex, *the ferocious* Allosaurus *is a common site in museum dinosaur halls. While* T-rex *remains are extremely rare, those of the* Allosaurus *are more plentiful. A large cache of* Allosaurus *skeletons has been uncovered at the Cleveland-Lloyd Quarry in Utah. Other fossil remains have been located elsewhere in the Rocky Mountain region as well as in Africa and Australia.*

As a theropod, the Allosaurus *is very remotely related to the similarly built, but larger* T-rex. *Keep in mind, however, that the two are separated by tens of millions of years on the dinosaur family tree. The* T-rex *appears in the fossil record about seventy million years ago, while the* Allosaurus *apparently died out more than sixty million years earlier.*

Jurassic animals under conditions likely to preserve their skeletons as fossils.

Indeed, when Douglass dug into the Uinta Morrison outcroppings, he immediately began to uncover huge bones. These turned out to be the vertebrae of a giant sauropod and, in time, would prove to be part of one of the most complete *Apatosaurus* skeletons ever discovered. Many more important finds were to follow. Over the next fifteen years, Douglass continued his painstaking excavations, eventually unearthing more than 350 tons of fossils including the remains of *Camarasaurus*, *Diplodocus*, *Barosaurus*, *Allosaurus*, *Ceratosaurus*, *Torvosaurus*, *Camptosaurus*, *Dryosaurus*, *Stegosaurus*, and other denizens of the Jurassic.

Nowadays, you can see some of the fossils Douglass and others discovered here at the Dinosaur Quarry Visitor Center about seven miles north of Jenson, Utah. The most extraordinary feature here is the dramatic exhibit of more than 1,600 dinosaur bones covering one entire wall of the center. The fossilized bones have been left in their natural state just as they looked when they were uncovered by paleontologists. The onsite laboratory where quarried fossils are cleaned and prepared for exhibit is open to the public.

Dinosaur Quarry is the chief, though by no means only, attraction of Dinosaur National Monument, which has its headquarters in Dinosaur, Colorado. This dino-hunter's paradise is enormous, encompassing more than 210,000 acres, and it offers endless opportunities to learn and explore. From the monument headquarters a sixty-two-mile roundtrip drive along Harpers Corner Road will take you on a "Journey Through Time," and some of the West's most spectacular scenery. Parking areas along the drive provide breathtaking views and access to trails offering close examination of the region's unique geology, flora, and fauna. From the Quarry Visitor Center just across the border in

Utah, a seventeen-mile roundtrip drive features Native American petroglyphs, the historic Morris homestead center, and additional trails.

One of the best ways to experience Dinosaur National Monument and its prehistoric riches is by water along the tumbling Green and Yampa Rivers. Check with the National Park Service by phone or access the monument Web site for the names and numbers of commercial white-water guides.

> Dinosaur National Monument
> 4545 Highway 40
> Dinosaur, CO 81610
> (970) 374-3000

or

> Dinosaur National Monument
> P.O. Box 128
> Jensen, UT 84035
> (435) 789-2115
> **www.nps.gov/dino**

Dinosaur Valley Museum

The Dinosaur Valley Museum is one of several display facilities associated with the Museum of Western Colorado in Grand Junction. Visitors will see dinosaur skeletons articulated in their "death pose" exactly as they were found in the field by paleontologists. To the delight of young and old alike there are also animated dinosaur models that move and roar. Serious students of paleontology will appreciate the on-site fossil laboratory.

The museum's extensive fossil collection includes numerous plant and marine species as well as land carnivores and plant-eaters. Largest of the museum's display fossils is that of a half-grown *Camarasaurus*, a plant-eating species believed to swallow large stones to help it grind and digest food. Although this one is smaller, some *Camarasaurus* skeletons are nearly sixty feet long.

Of major interest to dino-hunters are the public "Day Digs" and "Major Expeditions" organized by the museum. For a small fee you can participate in single-day outings to gather fossils in local areas or weeklong digs in well-known fossil quarries where the remains of giants such as the *Allosaurus* and *Apatosaurus* abound.

> Dinosaur Valley Museum
> 362 West Main Street
> P.O. Box 20000
> Grand Junction, CO 81502
> (970) 243-3466
> (888) 488-DINO
> **www.mwc.mus.co.us/dinosaurs**

Petrified Forest National Park

The Petrified Forest and nearby Painted Desert are part of the same park and together they encompass more than 93,500 acres of magical western landscape. The barren, rock-strewn hillsides and canyons here glow with bands of bright color, the exposed mineralogical evidence of 250 million years of natural history.

The massive, stony logs for which the park is named date to the Triassic, near the beginning of the Dinosaur Age. When they were living, approximately 225 million years ago, these giant trees looked much like modern Norfolk Island Pines and formed a great forest soaring more than 250 feet into the sky. The trees were felled by some natural cataclysm such as a major volcanic eruption or flood and then buried by silt. Over the years the once-living cells in the wood were slowly filled with rocky minerals forming the petrified logs we see today.

At the time the forest was destroyed and covered over, this part of Arizona was a vast swamp, alive with lush vegetation and crawling with reptiles such as the crocodile-like phytosaur. Among the creatures inhabiting this Triassic landscape was the meat-eating *Staurikosaurus*, a very small and very early ancestor of the *T-rex*. The fossilized bones of an eight-foot-tall *Staurikosaurus* unearthed in the park are among the oldest complete dinosaur skeletons ever found, and paleontologists have nicknamed it "Gertie." Currently, Gertie is under careful study by scientists, but she will eventually be placed on display at the

A LATE JURASSIC *carnivore, the* Ceratosaurus *lived at about the same time as the* Allosaurus *and was similar in many respects. At roughly twenty feet in length it was much smaller than the* Allosaurus, *but its razor-sharp claws and bladelike teeth would have made it a formidable predator, especially when hunting in a pack. The male* Ceratosaurus *had a hornlike bump on its snout. Shaped like the horn of a rhinoceros, it may have been used in combat with competing predators or, perhaps, in fights with other* Ceratosaurus *males for possession of females.*

CERATOSAURUS

park's Rainbow Forest Museum. This excellent facility contains many dinosaur fossils and dioramas depicting the area as it might have looked hundreds of millions of years ago when its forest grew tall.

But perhaps the most important study dino-hunters can make here is of the petrified wood, which lies tumbled and broken at the side of walking trails leading from the museum and visitors center. The beautiful, multicolored mineralized wood dramatically illustrates the forces that turn living matter to stone and preserve the shape and form of incredibly old living matter so that it can be studied today.

Since all fossils are valuable to our own as well as future generations, those here should be left intact and not be wantonly plundered. Unfortunately, thoughtless visitors walk off with several tons of the park's petrified wood every year. Please leave the wood in the park where everyone can see and enjoy it.

Petrified Forest National Park
P.O. Box 2217
Petrified Forest National Park, AZ 86028
(520) 524-6228
www.nps.gov/pefo

Wyoming Dinosaur Center

For the serious and even not so serious dino-hunter, the Wyoming Dinosaur Center is Mecca, a place requiring at least one major pilgrimage. Few dinosaur attractions anywhere in the world have so much to offer as this complex of museums and dig sites near Thermopolis, Wyoming.

The museum itself can boast of more than twelve thousand square feet of display space with perhaps a dozen major paleontology exhibitions. These take visitors on a journey through billions of years of prehistory from the remote Precambrian era down through the Mesozoic and Cenozoic Eras to our own time. Dioramas depict the earth in a series of stages as life developed over the ages.

Of course, the Mesozoic displays are the most fascinating part of the museum for those interested in dinosaurs. Here one sees fossils of *Triceratops*, *Apatosaurus*, *Utahraptor*, *Allosaurus*, *Tyrannosaurus rex*, *Ceratosaurus*, and literally dozens of other dinosaur or reptile species. There are dinosaur fossils from England, China, and throughout the American West as well as from digs at or near the center itself. Many are full-size mounted skeletons.

A substantial portion of the fossil material at the museum has been recovered from quarries on the Warm Springs Ranch near the museum. More than one thousand specimens have been unearthed at these productive sites, which have produced fossil evidence of *Diplodocus*, *Apatosaurus*, *Stegosaurus*, *Allosaurus*, *Camarasaurus*, *Camptosaurus*, and other dinosaurs. Most such specimens are processed at on-site fossil laboratories, which can be viewed by the public. The center also offers tours of the quarries.

Perhaps the center's most exciting attraction is its "Dig for a Day" program allowing visitors to get their hands dirty recovering dinosaur fossils. Participants may help excavate, stabilize, and document fossil discoveries.

> Wyoming Dinosaur Center
> P.O. Box 868
> Thermopolis, WY 82443
> (307) 864-2997
> (800) 455-DINO
> **www.wyodino.org**

73

FAR WEST

California Academy of Sciences

Founded in 1853, the California Academy of Sciences in San Francisco was originally intended for study of California's own vast natural resources, but its focus soon enlarged to encompass the globe. Today, it is the oldest scientific organization in the West, and its natural history museum one of the ten largest in the world. The Academy attracts more than 1.5 million visitors each year.

A world-class educational complex, the Academy consists of three separate facilities: the Steinhart Aquarium, the Morrison Planetarium, and the Natural History Museum. Naturally, the latter is the place for dino-hunters, and there they will find articulated skeletons of vicious meat-eaters such as *Allosaurus*, *Dilophosaurus*, and public enemy number one, *Tyrannosaurus rex*. The Academy's extensive fossil holdings and state-of-the-art displays place this museum on a par with the Smithsonian in Washington, D.C. and the American Museum of Natural History in New York. Since the museum provides an excellent overview, it is a good place for westerners to begin their dino safaris.

The hall to aim for is right at the front of the museum—with those big, ferocious skeletons, you can't miss it. Called "Life Through Time," the exhibition in this hall takes visitors on a 4.5-billion-year journey through the earth's turbulent history. You can spend an entire afternoon here, so plan accordingly.

Keep in mind that the museum has many other halls and offerings that you won't want to miss. With its mounted giraffe, gorilla, and other animals, the "African Safari" is especially attractive. So, too, is the Gem and Mineral Hall, which contains more than a thousand specimens including gold nuggets from the California Gold Rush and a 1,350-pound quartz crystal from Arkansas. In the Gary Larson Hall, the well-known cartoonist pokes fun at science, scientists, ordinary folks, himself, and— even dinosaurs.

Before your visit, you should check out the museum's offerings by means of a virtual tour on the Internet. Like several other California natural history museums, this one maintains an excellent Web site loaded with information, graphics, and photographs. It can be accessed through the Internet address.

California Academy of Sciences
Golden Gate Park
San Francisco, CA 94118
(415) 750-7145
www.calacademy.org

Natural History Museum of Los Angeles

One of the finest museums in the world, this natural history showplace can keep eager minds enraptured for days. Its exhibits on sharks, birds, gems, and Native American cultures are rated among the best anywhere. The same can be said for its paleontology displays, which of course, are of major interest to dino-hunters. Among the many permanent dinosaur exhibits are a complete skeleton cast of *Mamenchisaurus* (a Late Jurassic sauropod with an extremely long neck) and dramatic full-size models of *Allosaurus* and *Carnotaurus* (an Early Cretaceous meat-eater). Especially impressive is an enormous *Tyrannosaurus rex* skull, one of the few on view in any public museum.

Like the Museum of Paleontology in Berkeley, this facility also offers exciting on-line Internet exhibits. The dinosaur exhibit features *Albertosaurus*, *Apatosaurus*, *Euoplocephalus*, *Tenontosaurus*, and many other denizens of the Mesozoic era.

> Natural History Museum of Los Angeles
> 900 Exposition Boulevard
> Los Angeles, CA 90007
> (213) 744-3466
> **www.nhm.org**

Pacific Science Center

Located in Seattle Center not far from the famed Space Needle, the Pacific Science Center fills a complex of six buildings that once served as the United States Pavilion at the 1962 Seattle World's Fair. Its mission is much the same as that of the original pavilion—to charge the minds of children and adults with wonder and scientific curiosity and send them out to explore the cosmos for themselves. Through a combination of interpretive exhibits, planetarium programs, Imax movies, laser shows, and classes, the center brings the world of science to the people of the Northwest.

At the heart of the center are its exhibit halls where displays on high technology and robotics, health and the human body, hydrology, mechanics, and tidal pools, touch on nearly every field of science. But, of course, most popular is the prehistory exhibition, since that's dinosaur country. Called "Journey Through Time," it offers one of the liveliest dinosaur displays in America. Here, the center has re-created a lush, semitropical Mesozoic environment and filled it with five moving, roaring robotic dinos. Featured are full-size models of *Apatosaurus*, *Stegosaurus*, *Triceratops*, *Tyrannosaurus rex*, and *Pachycephalosaurus* (a Late Cretaceous plant-eater with a very thick skull). All these dinos are true-to-life and take the latest scientific discoveries and thinking into consideration.

The center's Web site is exceptionally colorful and informative. Its on-line exhibits are among the best on the Internet.

Pacific Science Center
200 Second Avenue North
Seattle, WA 98109
(206) 443-2001
www.pacsci.org

CANADA

Calgary Prehistory Park

Dinosaurs at the zoo? That seems unlikely since they've been extinct for sixty-five million years, but at the Calgary Zoo you can see dozens of dinos and other prehistoric animals in surroundings resembling their original habitats. The zoo's amazing Prehistoric Gardens consists of more than eighty acres landscaped with rocks and more than 120 species of plants to give the illusion of a Mesozoic scene.

A walk through the garden takes you through 160 million years of earth history from the beginning of the Triassic, about 225 million years ago, down through the end of the Cretaceous. Practically every step reveals a different dinosaur model. You will see Triceratops, *Tyrannosaurus rex*, *Apatosaurus*, *Edmontosaurus*, *Corythosaurus*, *Stegosaurus*, *Styracosaurus*, *Ankylosaurus*, *Struthiomimus*, *Ornitholestes*, and many other dinosaurs or prehistoric reptiles. There are also marine species such as *Elasmosaurus* and flying reptiles the likes of *Pteranodon*.

Of course there is a regular zoo here as well and a lush botanical garden to boot. One of the zoo's favorite attractions is Kamala, an Asian elephant that paints colorful pictures with a brush. Kamala's work may look a bit too modern for the tastes of some art lovers, but Jackson Pollack fans will love it.

The Calgary Zoo offers a number of *Zoofari Tours* each year to exotic locations such as the East African plains or the Galápagos Islands. Because they provide excellent opportunities to study natural history and evolution, these may be of interest to dino-hunters.

Calgary Prehistory Park
Calgary Zoo, Botanical Park, and Prehistoric Garden
P.O. Box 3036, Station B
Calgary, Alberta, Canada T2M 4R8
(403) 232-9300
(800) 588-9993
www.calgaryzoo.ab.ca

Canadian Museum of Nature

Two whole floors in the museum's Victoria Building are devoted to a permanent exhibition called "Life Through the Ages." That is where you'll find the dinosaurs, and there are quite a few of them—more than two thousand dinosaur fossils are displayed here. Among the best exhibits are skeleton mounts, models, or fossil specimens of *Triceratops, Anchiceratops* (another horned plant-eater), *Styracosaurus, Daspletosaurus,* and *Panaplosaurus* (a type of ankylosaur). The museum is very proud of its scientifically up-to-date reproductions.

Completed in 1905, the Edwardian Victoria Building has been nicknamed "the castle." The Canadian Parliament once met here in what is now the Hall of Invertebrates. Incidentally, this museum has its own resident ghost.

Canadian Museum of Nature
240 McLeod Street
Ottawa, Ontario, Canada K1P 6P4
(613) 566-4700
www.nature.ca

A FEROCIOUS MEAT-EATER, the Daspletosaurus *("Frightful Lizard") was built something like an* Albertosaurus *or* Tyrannosaurus *and lived at about the same time, the Late Cretaceous. It had a huge head and daggerlike teeth. Its powerful jaws probably worked something like a giant nutcracker—just right for crushing the thick bony plates of ankylosaurs or similarly armored prey.* Daspletosaurus *fossils are extremely rare and have been found only in Alberta, Canada.*

DASPLETOSAURUS

Dinosaur Provincial Park

Stretched out along the Red Deer River in central Alberta is Dinosaur Provincial Park. Preserved within its boundaries are some of the richest fossil resources in North America. Complete and partial skeletons of dozens of dinosaur species have been recovered here. The fossil-bearing formations date from the Late Cretaceous about seventy-five million years ago, at which time the climate in this area was not very Canadian at all. Instead, it was much more like that of northern Florida today. Rivers flowed eastward toward a shallow sea, and their warm, swampy floodplains provided a perfect environment for dinosaurs.

After more than a century of excavation by paleontologists from throughout the world, the Deer River site has produced more than 150 complete skeletons and thousands of assorted fossils from disorganized concentrations called bone beds.

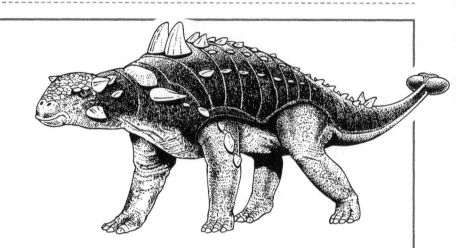

*B*UILT SOMETHING *like a modern battle tank, the thirty-foot-long* Ankylosaurus *was armored by a thick layer of bony plates covering its back. Weighing as much as four tons, it could probably ignore most predators, but when threatened was well equipped to fight back. Even the hungriest meat-eater would not have wanted to be hit with the heavy club at the end of an* Ankylosaurus *tail.*

ANKYLOSAURUS

Among the species found in the park are *Albertosaurus, Ornithomimus, Centrosaurus, Corythosaurus, Lambeosaurus, Elmisaurus* (a Late Cretaceous theropod), *Stegoceras* (a small, Late Cretaceous plant-eater), *Kritosaurus* (a Cretaceous duckbill), *Styracosaurus* (a four-legged, bird-hipped plant-eater with head spikes), and many others. More than a few of the best finds are now on display at Calgary's famed Royal Tyrrell Paleontology Museum. Others can be seen at the park visitors center.

Beyond the visitors center, a series of trails provides a first-hand view of the excavations and surrounding landscape. These badlands, with their valley walls, hills, and hoodoos (rocky pillars left behind by melting ice) are as much the product of the Ice Age, which ended about thirteen thousand years ago, as they are of the Cretaceous, which produced the local sands and dinosaur fossils.

> Dinosaur Provincial Park
> P.O. Box 60
> Patricia, Alberta, Canada T0J 2K0
> (403) 378-4342
> www.gov.ab.ca/env/parks/prov_parks/dinosaur

Royal Ontario Museum

Until 1955 the Royal Ontario operated as five distinct museums under the wing of the University of Toronto. Afterward, the archaeology, geology, mineralogy, zoology, and paleontology collections of these museums were combined to form the single, significant museum we know today. All together, the Royal Ontario now houses more than six million specimens and artifacts. While only a small fraction of this huge collection is on display, the museum's 200,000 square feet of floor space is crammed with fascinating exhibits. Doing justice to it all presents a formidable challenge to even the most determined museum-goer.

The entire second floor of the museum's main building is devoted to the Life Sciences and Paleontology Galleries, which provide visitors with an overview of the vast diversity of life on our planet. Since prehistory plays the principal role in this story, considerable space is devoted to it. Naturally enough, dinosaurs are the stars of the show. Mounted skeletons take center stage in colorful dioramas, the most dynamic of which are found in the Jurassic section. There an *Albertosaurus* towers menacingly, a *Chasmosaurus* pauses beside an actual dinosaur trackway, and a *Stegosaurus* stands his ground against a hungry *Allosaurus* while a nearby *Camptosaurus* runs for his life. You'll also see plesiosaurs, mosasaurs, and a host of other creatures from both the Mesozoic and Cenozoic periods. Other exhibits in this part of the museum focus on evolution, insects, bats, mammals, and birds.

To construct its prehistory exhibits the museum has been able to draw on its extensive fossil collections. Especially strong are its collections of Late Cretaceous dinosaurs from Alberta, Cretaceous and Tertiary vertebrates from Alberta and Saskatchewan, and Ice Age mammals from throughout the Americas. The Royal Ontario Museum continues to sponsor fossil-gathering expeditions all over the world.

> Royal Ontario Museum
> Main Building
> 100 Queen's Park
> Toronto, Ontario, Canada M5S 2C6
> (416) 586-5549
> www.rom.on.ca

Royal Tyrrell Museum of Paleontology

Located right in the middle of Canada's dinosaur country, this world-famous museum is one of North America's premier prehistory attractions. If you are serious about dinosaurs, the Tyrrell is a place you must see. In fact, like the American Museum of Natural History and several other places mentioned in this chapter, it would serve as an excellent place to begin your dino safari.

Dozens of mounted skeletons can be seen here. Among them are *Tyrannosaurus, Ornitholestes, Corythosaurus, Lam-*

*L*IKE SIMILAR *crested duckbills, such as* Cory-thosaurus *and* Parasaurolophus, *the Cretaceous plant-eater* Lambeosaurus *probably used its crest as a sort of trumpet. The animal's loud hooting might have served to attract mates or to warn its herd that danger was approaching. Considering the size, speed, and ferocity of the meat-eaters that fed on these relatively docile creatures, use of the crests as a long-distance signaling device makes plenty of sense.*

LAMBEOSAURUS

beosaurus, *Hadrosaurus, Centrosaurus, Coelophysis,* and many others. The *Albertosaurus* (named for the province) you'll see here is the best-preserved example of this *Tyrannosaurus*-like meat-eater yet found in Alberta.

The Tyrrell provides visitors with a solid grounding in science and geology before plunging them into the complex world of paleontology. A series of exhibits explains how fossils were created by natural processes and how they are carefully recovered by scientists. Visitors are taken on imaginary tours of digs such as the Dinosaur Provincial Park in nearby Patricia or the Lake Wapiti area in British Columbia where Tyrrell scientists have made many key discoveries. A large window wall offers a glimpse of the Tyrrell laboratory where important fossils are prepared.

The Tyrrell Web site, listed first among the recommended addresses below, is one of the best and most informative on the Internet. The virtual tour will take you not only on a step-by-step walk through the museum, but on a journey through the 4.5-billion-year history of the earth itself. The tour and other Web site features provide a wealth of useful information on the science of paleontology. Don't miss it.

> Royal Tyrrell Museum of Paleontology
> P.O. Box 7500
> Drumheller, Alberta, Canada T0J 0Y0
> (403) 823-7707
> **www.tyrrellmuseum.com**

Dinos in
New England

Connecticut State Museum of Natural History

Some of Connecticut's noted dinosaur tracks have made their way to this museum on the campus at the University of Connecticut. They join an impressive plesiosaur cast and a number of worthy fossils.

> Connecticut State Museum of Natural History
> University of Connecticut
> Box U-23
> Storrs, CT 06269
> (860) 486-4460
> **www.mnh.uconn.edu/species.htm**

Dinosaur State Park

Although it may come as a surprise to many, Connecticut is definitely dinosaur country. However, the state is known more for the extraordinary trackways found here than for its fossils. Probably the finest dinosaur trackway in the East can be found at Dinosaur State Park in Rocky Hill. Early settlers in these parts believed the three-toed tracks were left by an

86

extinct race of giant chickens—not a bad guess when you think about it.

Scientists believe the Rocky Hill tracks were made by *Dilophosaurus* about 185 million years ago. The *Dilophosaurus* was a medium-size Jurassic carnivore, which, incidentally, put in an appearance in the Speilberg/Creighton thriller *Jurassic Park*.

For those of us who prefer the real thing to fictional dinosaurs, this park is itself a thriller, since it provides dramatic visual evidence that dinosaurs once passed this way—and left their marks. Some of the tracks are now protected by a domed building containing a number of related fossils and exhibits. Visitors who bring plaster are allowed to make their own castings of dinosaur footprints.

> Dinosaur State Park
> West Street
> Rocky Hill, CT 06067
> (860) 529-8423
> **www.acorn-online.com/100dino.htm**

Powder Hill Dinosaur Park

With its high-steepled churches and quiet streets, the town of Middlefield, Connecticut, seems an unlikely place to hunt for dinosaurs. Appearances, however, can be deceiving. In this lovely village, a few miles south of Hartford, is a small park containing unmistakable evidence that Jurassic giants once lived here. Left perhaps 150 million years ago, these heavy footprints are among several well-known dinosaur trackways in Connecticut. To come across them in the bucolic New England countryside is an experience not to be missed. Powder Hill Park has no full-time attendant so please be mindful of other visitors, take nothing away, and leave nothing but your own footprints.

Powder Hill Dinosaur Park
Town of Middlefield
Middlefield, CT 06455
(860) 349-7116

MAINE

Children's Museum of Maine

In addition to the usual prehistoric fossils and models one expects to see in a children's museum, this Portland Maine educational facility offers a collection of fossil replicas that kids can handle and study for themselves. For small children, the hands-on approach to dinosaurs is nearly always best.

Children's Museum of Maine
142 Free Street
Portland, ME 04101
(207) 828-1234
www.childrensmuseumofme.org

Maine State Museum

During the last 100,000 years, vast sheets of ice swept over Maine and much of New England, scrubbing rocks clean of fossils left here during the Age of Dinosaurs. For this reason and others, most of the prehistoric remains found in this state are those of Ice Age creatures such as the mammoth. Visitors to the state museum on the capitol grounds in Augusta will see mammoth bones and a worthy array of other Ice Age fossils.

Maine State Museum
State House Complex
Augusta, ME 04333
(207) 287-2301

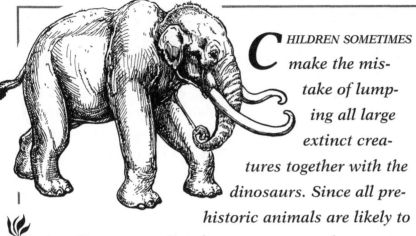

MAMMOTH

*C*HILDREN SOMETIMES *make the mistake of lumping all large extinct creatures together with the dinosaurs. Since all prehistoric animals are likely to be of interest to dino-hunters, mammoths, mastodons, saber-toothed cats, and a number of other extinct Cenozoic mammals are mentioned in this book. It is important, however, to keep in mind that most of these animals are separated by millions of years from the dinosaurs. In fact, some, such as the elephant-like mammoth and mastodon, were a familiar sight to Ice Age humans, who may very well have hunted them to extinction.*

MASTODON

MASSACHUSETTS

Boston Museum of Science

Located in Boston's Back Bay area, the Museum of Science offers a quiet and thought-provoking escape from the traffic and hubbub of the city center. Traffic congestion was not a major problem back in 1830 when a group of avid local amateur naturalists founded Boston Natural History Society. Eventually, their wide-ranging collections were drawn together into a museum located on Berkeley Street in the Back Bay. Following World War Two, the museum was moved to its present site beside what is now known as Science Park.

Visitors will find much to enjoy in this museum, since nearly every field of science receives some attention here. But for dino-hunters the highlight is likely to be the museum's recently acquired skull of *Giganotosaurus*, the humongous *T-rex*-type meat-eater discovered recently in Argentina's Northern Patagonia desert. The skull is six-feet long and brandishes rows of daggerlike teeth capable of biting off half a ton of flesh at a time. The *Giganotosaurus* grew up to forty-five feet in length and weighed in at between eight and ten tons. This hungry fellow was not something you would want to meet on a dark Back Bay street, in a San Diego filling station, or anywhere else, for that matter. The *Giganotosaurus* joins a one-and-a-half-story *Tyrannosaurus* model, a mounted *Triceratops* skeleton, *Apatosaurus* footprints from a trackway in Texas, and an array of other dinosaur fossils, casts, and models.

For extra excitement check out the Science Museum's educational travel programs featuring excursions to exotic spots such as the Galápagos and Sahara. And don't miss the exciting on-line exhibits accessible through the Web site listed on page 92.

*P*ROBABLY ALL *dinosaurs descended from a common ancestor, but what was it? Since the fossil record is incomplete and very hard to read, it may be impossible to identify the first dinosaur. Even so, some very early dinosaurs have been found. One of these is the* Herrerasaurus, *a theropod found in the Ischigualisto Formation of Argentina. A bipedal carnivore, it dates back far into the Triassic and may have killed and eaten prey as long as 230 million years ago. Not nearly as big as many of the dinosaurs that would follow, it weighed a little more than 220 pounds or about as much as a blocking back for a college football team.*

With its wide-open desert country, deep canyons, and rugged mountains, Argentina resembles the western U.S. in some respects, and like the West, has proved a very productive place to look for dinosaur fossils. Recently, fossils of Giganotosaurus, *a meat-eater of tremendous size, were found there. Perhaps the ten-ton* Giganotosaurus, *which lived toward the end of the Age of Dinosaurs, was a descendant of the much smaller* Herrerasaurus, *which lived 160 million years earlier.*

G I G A N T O S A U R U S

HERRERASAURUS

Boston Museum of Science
Science Park
Boston, MA 02114
(617) 723-2500
www.mos.org

Dinosaur Footprints Reservation

Among the several known dinosaur trackways in the Connecticut Valley, this is a standout. More than one species of
dinosaur left their marks here, including a few very large meat-
eaters. Those planning a visit should check with the reservation office listed below for directions and other information.
Visitors should consider the importance of this prehistoric
treasure and take great care not to damage it. Removing fossils
from the site is illegal.

Dinosaur Footprints Reservation
P.O. Box 792
Stockbridge, MA 01262
(413) 298-3239

Nash Dinosaur Museum

A small, private paleontology museum and gift shop in South
Hadley, Massachusetts, the Nash is a great place to buy some
fossils for your personal collection. A fossil quarry located on
the museum grounds is worked primarily by Carleton Nash, an
amateur paleontologist, fossil aficionado, and the museum's
owner. About forty years ago, Nash discovered five rare
dinosaur footprints on the property, and he has been fascinated
by fossils and the subject of paleontology ever since. In other
words, he's a dino-hunter.

Nash Dinosaur Museum
Amherst Road (Route 116)
South Hadley, MA 01075
(413) 467-9566

Pratt Museum of Natural History

With the exception of the Peabody Museum at Yale and Harvard's Museum of Comparative Zoology, you won't find more or better vertebrate fossils anywhere in New England than those at the Pratt. Amherst College has offered a strong science curriculum since the 1820s, and it was among the first educational institutions to pursue prehistoric vertebrate zoology. The fossil collection at Amherst's Pratt Museum has been growing for the better part of two centuries, and as a result, it is now one of the best anywhere.

As you enter the museum, you are greeted by three enormous elephantine skeletons—a mammoth, a mastodon, and a modern Indian elephant. Nearby are a saber-toothed cat, Irish elk, moa, and cave bear, all of them species that have become extinct only in the last few thousand years. The likely role played by humans in the loss of these species will not be lost on perceptive visitors. Extinction, both prehistoric and recent, is an important theme here. So, too, is evolution. A famous exhibit at the Pratt illustrates the evolution of the modern horse from a small forest-dwelling creature fifty-five million years, through early and intermediate forms such as *Mesohippus* and *Merychippus*, down to our own grass-dwelling *Equus*.

The Pratt features plenty of dinosaurs. Fossil displays include *Triceratops*, *Tyrannosaurus rex*, *Diplodocus*, the duck-billed *Kritosaurus*, and many other species. Early amphibians and mammals are also well represented. Incidentally, the Pratt's Web site is highly informative and well worth a cyber-visit.

Pratt Museum of Natural History
Amherst College
Amherst, MA 01103
(413) 542-2165
www.amherst.edu/~pratt

Springfield Science Museum

Springfield's Science Museum is part of a substantial complex of four handsome public buildings arranged around a tree-lined quadrangle in the very heart of the city. The other buildings house the Connecticut Valley Historical Museum, George Walter Vincent Smith Art Museum, and Springfield City Library. The quadrangle is a great place to spend a spare Saturday or Sunday afternoon, although visitors may have difficulty deciding how to invest their hours. For dino-hunters, the decision will be an easy one since the Science Museum makes no secret of its full-size models or mounted skeletons of *Tyrannosaurus rex*, *Stegosaurus*, and *Coelophysis* (a late Triassic meat-eater). Many of the exhibits in Dinosaur Hall and elsewhere in this museum are of the hands-on variety, which makes this a great place to bring children. Don't miss the African Hall with its spectacular dioramas or Mineral Hall with its fascinating gems and geodes. Kids will love the hands-on Exploration Center.

Springfield Science Museum
220 State Street
Springfield, MA 01103
(413) 236-6800
www.quadrangle.org

Wistariahusrt Museum

Perhaps it is not entirely fair to describe Holyoke's wonderful, old Wistariahurst mansion as a dinosaur, but in a positive

94

sense, the comparison certainly suggests itself. Like a friendly sauropod left over from the Jurassic, this time traveler from the late nineteenth century is endlessly fascinating. Built in 1875 by William Skinner, a wealthy silk merchant and manufacturer, the elaborate Victorian home is an exuberant expression of the times that created it. Much of the decoration and furnishing reflects the Beaux Arts movement and revival styling popular during the 1880s.

Today, the Wistariahurst serves as a unique museum focusing primarily on the history and styles of the late Victorian era. Surprisingly enough, however, there is something here of considerable interest to inveterate dino-hunters. On the grounds outside the mansion are the footprints of dinosaurs that passed through this area many millions of years ago. Flagstones used to build a covered porch at the back of the building contain tracks more than one hundred million years old.

Wistariahusrt Museum
238 Cabot Street
Holyoke, MA 01041
(413) 534-2216
www.holyoke.org/mainpage.htm

VERMONT

Montshire Museum of Science

The Montshire describes itself as a "hands-on museum," meaning that it is a wonderful place for kids. This Norwich museum offers dozens of well-conceived exhibits on ecology, technology, natural history, and science. Even the building itself was designed to serve as an exhibit with color-coded heating and ventilation ducts, a see-through elevator hoistway, and exposed trusses allowing visitors to see how the structure is supported. While the Ice Age glaciers carried away nearly all traces of dinosaur fossils from New England, the Montshire does have a few on display. Mostly they are used for purposes of comparison in a reptile exhibit.

Montshire Museum of Science
One Montshire Road
Norwich, VT 05055
(802) 649-2200
www.montshire.net

Dinos in the
Mid-Atlantic States

Calvert Cliffs State Park

During the Victorian era, "geologizing" was a popular hobby among members of society's upper crust who had the leisure time for such activities. Maryland's fossil-rich Calvert Cliffs State Park is just the sort of place amateur geologists would go to do their collecting. The cliffs here contain fossils representing six hundred distinct species dating back fifteen million years to Miocene times. Among the more popular finds are shark teeth. The often large and impressive teeth may survive more or less intact for millions of years after the rest of the shark's body has turned to clay. Happily, today's fossil prospectors are allowed to keep whatever they dig up here. This is a real attraction for families with kids looking for souvenir reminders of primordial ocean marauders.

> Calvert Cliffs State Park
> Point Lookout State Park
> P.O. Box 48
> Scotland, MD 20687
> (301) 872-5688
> **www.calvert-county.com/stateprk.htm**

Calvert Marine Museum

The maritime history of the Chesapeake Bay region is the primary concern of this Solomons, Maryland, museum. Among its highlights are an 1883 cottage-style lighthouse, a number of small, historic watercraft, a boat-building center, a model-making shop, an old oyster-packing house, and a historic waterman's residence. But because the museum is located near the fossil-rich Calvert Cliffs, paleontology plays an important role here as well. Side by side with the museum's two hundred-year-old maritime artifacts are twenty-million-year-old fossils.

Fittingly, most of the Calvert's fossils are of creatures that lived in or near the sea. Unique among the fossil displays is the skeleton of a *Pelagornis*, an extinct relative of today's pelicans and gannets. The *Pelagornis* had a serrated beak and an incredible wingspan of more than eighteen feet. The full-size skeleton now flies over the museum's recently expanded fossil hall called "Treasure from the Cliffs: Exploring Marine Fossils." The *Pelagornis* is also featured in a mural depicting the Chesapeake area as it may have looked fifteen million years ago. As with the Calvert Cliffs themselves, there is little or no dinosaur material to be found here, but the museum and fossils help open up and widen the world of paleontology for both the uninitiated and prehistory experts alike.

Calvert Marine Museum
P.O. Box 97
Solomons, MD 20688
(410) 326-2042
www.calvertmarinemuseum.com

NEW JERSEY

Morris Museum

Founded in 1913 as a small youth museum or learning center for local children, the Morris Museum in Morristown, New Jersey, has grown into an internationally recognized institution. The museum's first exhibits consisted of a few random items drawn from a community center curio cabinet. Today more than forty-eight thousand objects are included in its extraordinarily eclectic collections, which range from dinosaur fossils to children's' toys, from nineteenth-century household appliances to fine Oriental art. The museum attracts more than 300,000 schoolchildren and adults each year.

The museum's most popular exhibition is, of course, its Dinosaur and Fossil Gallery. Inside this spacious hall visitors will find 500-million-year-old trilobites from the Cambrian period. Not surprisingly, the gallery's most dramatic displays are from the Jurassic, which is well represented with a beautifully preserved *Ornitholestes* skeleton, *Stegosaurus* model, *Pteranodon* replica, and *Tyrannosaurus* skull. There are also dinosaur tracks drawn from various sites in New Jersey. The interactive Footprint Path exhibit allows you to compare your own footprints to those of several different dinosaur species.

When you visit the Morris, don't spend all your time with the dinosaurs. This fine museum offers many other delightful exhibitions including one of the finest Asian art collections in America.

Morris Museum
6 Normandy Heights Road
Morristown, NJ 07960
(973) 538-0454
www.morrismuseum.org

New Jersey State Museum

Established in 1895, this state-run museum offers collections, exhibits, and interpretive services in four broad areas: fine art, cultural history, archaeology and ethnology, and natural history. Located in Trenton, the facility includes a planetarium, an auditorium, and a four-level exhibit building. Dino-hunters will want to visit the latter as it contains considerable fossil material, much of it found in New Jersey.

While New Jersey is not widely known for its dinosaurs—at least not to the public—some of America's most important dinosaur finds were made in this state. Among these was a *Hadrosaurus* discovered on a farm near Haddonfield in 1858. The remains of this eight-ton, Cretaceous duck-billed plant-eater were dug from a clay pit and eventually mounted at the state museum in Trenton. There you can still see this historic

*W*ITH ITS *elongated skull and toothless beak, the* Pteranodon *looked something like a modern pelican. What is more, it likely lived off small fish, which it scooped out of the water much as pelicans do today. However, it is not clear how well these creatures could fly. Some think they were primarily gliders.*

PTERANODON

Hadrosaurus skeleton—among the first dinosaurs found in America—along with mounted mastodons and other prehistoric skeletons. Occasionally, the museum offers special dinosaur programs for children.

New Jersey State Museum
P.O. Box 530
205 West State Street
Trenton, NJ 08625
(609) 292-6464
www.state.nj.us/state/museum
www.nj.com/dino/museum.html

Princeton Natural History Museum

Noted paleontologist and dinosaur expert Jack Horner once worked at the Princeton Natural History Museum, which features a *Maiasaura* skeleton he discovered in Montana. Also on display are a mounted *Allosaurus* and *Tyrannosaurus* along with numerous other fossil materials. Mammal exhibits include fossils of the magnificent Irish elk, which became extinct in relatively recent times.

Princeton Natural History Museum
Guyot Halls
Washington Street
Princeton University
Princeton, NJ 08544
(609) 258-4102
www.princeton.edu

Rutgers University Geology Museum

Apparently, dinosaurs liked New Jersey, as they left a great many footprints in the state. Some of their trackways can be

H
A
D
R
O
S
A
U
R
U
S

*A*MONG THE *first dinosaur skeletons discovered in the United States was that of a* Hadrosaurus *uncovered near Haddonfield, New Jersey, in 1858. Described as a duck-billed dinosaur because of its flattened, shovel-shaped snout, the* Hadrosaurus *gave its name to an entire group of similar Late Cretaceous plant-eaters known as hadrosaurids. The* Hadrosaurus, *and other duckbills, such as the* Anatosaurus, Bactrosaurus, *and* Edmontosaurus, *were once thought to have lived in swamps. Later study showed that the duckbills ate pine needles and woody plants that grew in drier locales. Near the back of their jaws, they had rows of grinding teeth good for pulverizing coarse plant materials.*

seen at the Rutgers University Geology Museum in New Brunswick. Rock hounds won't want to miss the museum's massive cross section exhibit, depicting New Jersey from the Delaware Water Gap in the northeast all the way to the southern coastal plain. However, the holdings of this geology museum range well beyond the minerals and gemstones you might normally expect to see. For instance, among the notable displays here is a Ptolemaic Egyptian mummy.

In addition to the trackways, the museum offers a considerable variety of dinosaur fossils including a skull cast of an *Allosaurus* and a mounted skeleton of a *Maiasaura*. There is also a mastodon along with other prehistoric mammal remains. Much of the fossil material was found in New Jersey.

Rutgers University Geology Museum
College Avenue
New Brunswick, NJ 08903
(732) 258-4102
www.rutgers.edu

New York

Buffalo Museum of Science

Buffalo's Museum of Science can trace its beginning to 1861, the first year of the American Civil War. That is when a group of local naturalists founded the Buffalo Society of Natural Science. Members of the society were avid collectors, and before long, they had compiled so many bird, animal, and plant specimens that the rooms they rented were filled to overflowing. Seeking more space for its expanding collections, the society moved its specimens, first to the Buffalo Public Library and, eventually, into the handsome building where they are kept today. The 93,000-square-foot museum was completed in 1929, and it houses offices, laboratories, and classrooms. More than a third of the area is used for exhibits, so visitors have plenty of room to stretch their legs.

Dino-hunters likely will head straight to the dinosaur exhibition with its mounted skeletons, models, and numerous fossils. Life-size displays include *Allosaurus*, *Nanosaurus*, and *Triceratops*. Marine reptiles such as mosasaurs are also represented as well as early aviators such as the pterosaurs and *Archaeopteryx*.

Nowadays, museums are far more than just exhibit halls or warehouses for huge collections. They are continually searching for new ways to educate and expand public awareness of science and nature. This is being done partly on the Internet, and the Buffalo Museum of Science maintains a worthy Web site. But the museum has found another new and unique way to extend its educational mandate—it now serves as a magnet school for area students who attend classes in the building.

Buffalo Museum of Science
1020 Humbolt Parkway
Buffalo, NY 14211
(716) 896-5200
www.sciencebuff.org

Durham Center Museum

Much of the extensive fossil collection at the Durham Center once belonged to Vernon Haskin, an avid collector and expert on prehistory. Most of the 200- to 300-million-year-old fossils here are of plants and invertebrates that lived before the time of the dinosaurs. Museum exhibits are by no means limited to fossils, however. They include an 1825 schoolhouse and pioneer artifacts as well as genealogical records and resources.

Durham Center Museum
Route 145
East Durham, NY 12423
(518) 239-8461

New York State Museum

Founded during the mid-nineteenth century, the New York State Museum has been researching natural and human history for more than 160 years. These efforts have generated a vast collection of more than five million artifacts and specimens. Every known mammal, bird, plant, and fish found in New York is represented. Cultural materials documenting the history of agriculture, industry, and the decorative arts extend to more than 350,000 objects and more than a million photographs.

NOT TRUE dinosaurs, the pterosaurs were flying reptiles ranging in size from that of an ordinary sparrow to that of a small airplane. Pterosaurs had leathery wings attached to their arms and to lengthy finger extensions. Although paleontologists never doubted that they could take to the air, pterosaurs were long believed to have been primarily opportunistic gliders. It was thought they would use their sharp claws to climb cliff faces, from which they would fly in search of food or to avoid predators. More recent analysis, indicates that they likely flapped their wings and could lift themselves into the air much as birds do today. Pterosaurs lived throughout the Jurassic and Cretaceous, disappearing along with the dinosaurs about sixty-five million years ago.

PTEROSAURS

Not surprisingly, the museum's fossil collection is one of the largest in the world. In fact, the modern science of paleontology grew, in part, out of work conducted at this very museum. However, the dinosaur exhibits you will see here are not as numerous or impressive as those you'll find at some other large northeastern museums—for instance the American Museum of Natural History in New York City. They include fossils, dinosaur tracks, and a few articulated skeletons.

Among the museum's permanent exhibitions is an excellent series of displays on the "Adirondack Wilderness" from about four thousand years ago—not very far back at all in terms of geological time—to the present. The "Native Peoples of New

York" exhibition examines human life in the Hudson Valley from the days of the earliest Ice Age hunters through the Mohawk-Iroquois period. The "New York Metropolis" traces the growth and development of New York City from a wilderness to the time of skyscrapers. The Empire State still has plenty of living dinosaur species, and you may want to take a look at a few of them in the "Birds of New York" exhibition, which includes each of the 170 species commonly found here.

> New York State Museum
> Cultural Education Center
> Albany, NY 12230
> (518) 474-5877
> www.nysm.nysed.gov

Petrified Creatures Museum

Visitors to this private museum can dig for fossils and keep whatever they find. Most of the fossils are those of early sea creatures.

> Petrified Creatures Museum
> P.O. Box 751
> Richfield Springs, NY 13439
> (315) 858-2868
> www.cooperstownchamber.org/pcm

PENNSYLVANIA

Rennie Geology Museum

You won't see much in the way of dinosaurs here, but the museum does feature a comprehensive collection of trilobites. These three-lobed marine invertebrates dominated the world's oceans for millions of years. Their fossils are abundant in Paleozoic rocks and clays. Trilobites were long gone by the time dinosaurs appeared about 225 million years ago.

Rennie Geology Museum
Dickinson College
Carlisle, PA 17013
(717) 245-1448
www.dickinson.edu

Wagner Free Institute of Science

During the 1840s, philanthropist and gentleman scientist William Wagner began offering lectures on science at his home in Elm Grove just outside of Philadelphia. An enthusiastic collector, Wagner began to fill his stately Victorian mansion with natural history specimens and artifacts. Today, his home is a museum housing the more than 100,000 curios and items of scientific interest that he and others assembled here. Among them are mounted skeletons, skulls, skins, birds, shells, and fossils.

What should interest the visitor even more than the objects themselves is the way they are exhibited. The displays have changed little in the last century. Some of the display cases are antiques and of historical interest themselves. Items are laid out in logical order with simpler discoveries leading to more complex ones. The entire experience is an education in the Victorian view of the world, and that should be of considerable interest to dino-hunters. Victorian explorers and "gentlemen scientists" such as Wagner—or Dr. Gideon Mantell and his wife Mary (see pages 17)—were the first to bring dinosaurs to the attention of the world. Here at the Wagner house, you may see them through the eyes of Victorians.

Wagner Free Institute of Science
17th Street and Montgomery Avenue
Philadelphia, PA 19121
(215) 763-6529

Dinos in
the South

Alabama Museum of Natural History

Not everyone who visits the University of Alabama campus in Tuscaloosa comes here to see a football game. Some are in search of dinosaurs. At the Alabama Museum of Natural History in Smith Hall beside the historic campus quadrangle, visitors will find intriguing fossils dating from the Cretaceous period down through the Ice Age. Prominent among the museum's featured exhibits on ethnology, geology, and mineralogy is the Hodges Meteorite. This is the only meteorite known to have struck a person. Apparently, the dinosaurs were not the only ones threatened by chunks of rocks falling from the sky.

> Alabama Museum of Natural History
> P.O. Box 870340
> Tuscaloosa, AL 35487
> (205) 348-2040
> **www.ua.edu/musmain.htm**

Anniston Museum of Natural History

Anniston, Alabama, lies in the foothills of the Southern Appalachians, believed by many to be the oldest mountains on earth. So it is appropriate that Anniston's Museum of Natural History celebrates the 4.5-billion-year natural history of our planet. Among the museum's several fine galleries is one devoted to the "Dynamic Earth," which details the process of formation and shows how the planet has changed over the ages. Visitors can touch a meteorite, marvel at gemstones, and see fossilized remains of long-buried plants and animals that thrived millions of years ago. Of particular interest to dino-hunters is the *Pteranodon* (a flying reptile) shown swooping down to protect its young from attack by a hungry, 20-foot-long *Albertosaurus*.

Other handsome halls include "Underground Worlds," a man-made cave with dripping stalactites; "Attack and Defense," devoted to the deadly interplay between predator and prey; "Designs for Living," containing one of the nation's oldest bird dioramas; and "Adaptations to the Environment," which emphasizes lions, leopards, elephants, and other large African animals. The museum's attractions extend to the outdoors with a wildlife garden, bird-of-prey trail, nature trail, and mountaintop hiking trail.

The entrance to the museum features the enormous skull of a *Mosasaurus*, a fish-eating sea lizard now celebrated as Alabama's official state fossil. But those of us on dino safari may be even more fascinated by the museum's prehistoric bird diorama, which illustrates the link between dinosaurs and modern birds.

Anniston Museum of Natural History
800 Museum Drive
Anniston, AL 36202
(256) 237-6766
www.annistonmuseum.org

McWane Center

Birmingham's Red Mountain got its name from the ruddy seam of iron that runs through it. The rich ore mined here formed the basis of the steel industry that helped build this prosperous city. But there is a lot more to the mountain than iron. Construction crews that built the highways across the mountain had to blast and dig down through many layers of rock and, in doing so, laid bare hundreds of millions of years of earth history. The half-mile-long Red Mountain Road Cut offers dino-hunters a dynamic illustration of how rock layers pile up one atop the other over the eons. You can learn all about it at the city's sparkling new McWane Science Center in downtown Birmingham. The museum's indoor exhibits include a fifteen-foot articulated skeleton of *Mosasaurus*, an *Allosaurus* skull, and many marine fossils.

> McWane Center
> 200 19th Street North
> Birmingham, AL 35205
> (205) 714-8400
> www.mcwane.org

ARKANSAS

Arkansas Geological Commission & Learning Center

The exhibits at this state office in Little Rock are designed mostly to attract rock hounds or schoolkids and others interested in geology. However, there are some fascinating fossil displays and dinosaur models.

> Arkansas Geological Commission & Learning Center
> 3815 West Roosevelt Road
> Little Rock, AR 72204
> (501) 296-1877
> www.state.ar.us/agc/agc.htm

Arkansas Museum of Discovery

Formerly located in the old Little Rock Arsenal, best known as the birthplace of Gen. Douglas MacArthur, this museum has moved to the popular River Market District downtown. It contains a number of dinosaur attractions. Prominent among them is a life-size reproduction of an *Ornithomimus*, a birdlike Cretaceous carnivore that once roamed Arkansas and much of North America. The museum has many other paleontology exhibits including fossils and dinosaur tracks.

> Arkansas Museum of Discovery
> 500 East Markham
> Little Rock, AR 72201
> (501) 396-7050

Dinosaur World

Chances are you won't learn very much about paleontology here. If you don't mind camping out, however, you can sleep in the midst of several dozen life-size dinosaur replicas. Camping and fishing here are a bit like stepping onto the set of *Jurassic Park*. The kids will love it and so will you. After all—and as is pointed out elsewhere in this book—one of the wonderful things about dinosaurs is that they bring together the worlds of science and the imagination.

> Dinosaur World
> Route 2 Box 408
> Eureka Springs, AR 72632
> (501) 253-8113

Mountainburg Dinosaurs

Travelers passing through Mountainburg on U.S. Highway 71 can't help but notice the two enormous dinos that grace the city park. A local artisan crafted them using hundreds of bags of concrete. They're not much on realism, but they sure are a lot of fun.

Mountainburg Dinosaurs
City of Mountainburg
P.O. Box 433
Mountainburg, AR 72946
(501) 369-2791

Nashville County Dinosaur Tracks

The dinosaur tracks previously on display at the courthouse in Nashville, Arkansas, have been moved to the Nashville City Park. The tracks are only casts of the originals, but they are quite interesting. A mining operation accidentally uncovered the tracks

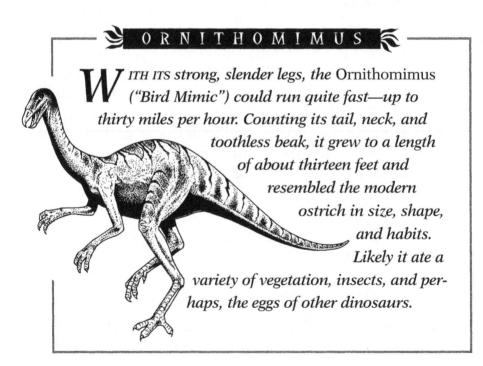

ORNITHOMIMUS

WITH ITS strong, slender legs, the Ornithomimus *("Bird Mimic") could run quite fast—up to thirty miles per hour. Counting its tail, neck, and toothless beak, it grew to a length of about thirteen feet and resembled the modern ostrich in size, shape, and habits. Likely it ate a variety of vegetation, insects, and perhaps, the eggs of other dinosaurs.*

some years ago and casts were made before the originals were destroyed. The tracks are those of many different dinosaurs, most of them as yet unidentified.

Nashville County Dinosaur Tracks
Nashville County Courthouse
421 North Main
Nashville, AR 71852
(501) 845-7500

University of Arkansas Museum

This small but rewarding campus museum contains a number of excellent fossil exhibits. One of these features an early crocodile-like creature that lived and captured its prey in the vast swamps that covered Arkansas during much of the dinosaur era. It is interesting to note that crocodiles still inhabit the planet, while the dinosaurs—except for birds—have vanished.

University of Arkansas Museum
202 Museum
Garland Street
Fayetteville, AR 72701
(501) 575-3466
www.uark.edu

FLORIDA

Brevard Museum of Natural History and Science

Most of the fossils on display at this small Florida museum are of the marine variety, so the dinosaur connection is rather thin. Still, as a natural history museum, it offers the sort of information useful in a wider search for dinos and other prehistoric wonders.

Brevard Museum of Natural History and Science
2201 Michigan Avenue
Cocoa, FL 32926
(407) 632-1830

Daytona Museum of Art and Science

As befitting a Museum in Daytona Beach, the fossil exhibits here focus on the sea. Even today, the highest point in Florida is only a few dozen feet above sea level. During Cambrian times and earlier, when dinosaurs walked the earth, Florida had no dry land at all. Still there were plenty of marine creatures and they left an abundance of fossils. Some fine examples can be seen at the museum.

Visitors should take advantage of the museum's other excellent displays. The anthropology and art sections are unusual and highly interesting. Among the best are exhibits on American art, Cuban art, Chinese art, and African culture.

Daytona Museum of Art and Science
1040 Museum Boulevard
Daytona Beach, FL 32114
(904) 255-0285
www.moas.org/museum.htm

Florida Museum of Natural History

This museum has the right stuff. With the opening of its exciting new exhibition center in Powell Hall, the Florida Museum of Natural History on the University of Florida Campus in Gainesville has pushed the museum-going experience into the twenty-first century and beyond. Its emphasis, although not always on dinosaurs and paleontology, has been put where it belongs—on the *investigation* of the world of science. More often than not, traditional museums have served as warehouses for specimens and artifacts. Powell Hall is a place to ask questions and learn about nature.

Nonetheless, the museum has plenty of artifacts and specimens, in fact, some nineteen million of them. The original museum exhibition center across the campus from the new one at Powell Hall is being redesigned to accommodate this rather overwhelming mass collection.

Dino-hunters will be particularly interested in the Florida Fossil exhibition near the entrance to Powell Hall. They will not, however, find many dinosaurs there. Florida had trouble keeping its head above water during much of the 160-million-year Age of Dinosaurs, and so fossils of land animals are quite rare in this state. On the other hand, the remains of sea creatures are abundant and the museum's marine fossil exhibits are among the best in the world.

Perhaps the most attractive facility at the museum is its Center for Natural History Investigation, which is still under development. When complete, the center will offer multimedia libraries, banks of computers for in-depth, on-line research, and mentors to help curious children and adults find their way to the truth. Equipment such as microscopes, soil and water analysis kits, and observation chambers can be checked out for use outdoors.

> Florida Museum of Natural History
> Museum Road
> Gainesville, FL 32611
> (352) 392-1721 or (352) 846-2967
>
> Florida Museum of Natural History (Powell
>   Exhibition Center)
> Powell Hall
> Hull Road and Southwest 34th Street
> Gainesville, FL 32611
> **www.flmnh.ufl.edu**

Jacksonville Museum of Science and History

Interactive displays make Jacksonville's Museum of Science and History especially fun for children. The natural history holdings concentrate on local and marine fossils. However, there is an exciting *Allosaurus* skeleton on hand to greet and frighten visitors. Meat-eating dinosaurs of this type grew to thirty feet or more in length and are thought to have hunted in ferocious packs. A particularly worthwhile feature of this museum is its "Ribbon of Life" exhibit, which explores the history and ecology of the Saint John's River.

> Jacksonville Museum of Science and History
> 1025 Museum Circle
> Jacksonville, FL 32207
> (904) 396-MOSH
> www.jacksonvillemuseum.com

Mulberry Phosphate Fossil Museum

Earlier in this century, mining companies strip-mined and shipped millions of tons of Florida phosphates for use in fertilizers and industry. In the process, miners uncovered many fossils. Although most were discarded or destroyed, a few made their way into museums such as this one in the small town of Mulberry. Like most Florida fossils, these reflect the marine environment of the primordial seas that covered Florida throughout much of the earth's history.

> Mulberry Phosphate Fossil Museum
> P.O. Box 707
> Mulberry, FL 33860
> (941) 425-2823

Museum of Florida History

Since this is primarily a history museum, its substantial collections focus on things such as citrus labels and Civil War flags. Even so, those entering the museum will be greeted by a twelve-foot-high mounted mastodon with formidable tusks. It's not a dinosaur, of course, but it is impressive. The museum offers a number of other worthy fossil exhibits.

Museum of Florida History
500 South Bronough Street
Tallahassee, FL 32399
(850) 488-1484
www.dos.state.fl.us/dhr/museum

Naples Conservancy Nature Center

The Conservancy's Nature Science Museum features a number of handsome dioramas. Some contain fossils, and dino-hunters may think they are worth a look. Even more worthwhile, however, are the Center's nature trails and other outdoor attractions that provide access to Florida's lush environment. To those of us with active imaginations, the Florida landscape suggests Mesozoic times, when enormous sauropods tromped though marshes perhaps not unlike these.

Naples Conservancy Nature Center
1450 Merrihue Drive
Naples, FL 34102
(941) 262-0304
www.conservancy.org

Universal Studios Florida

The Universal Studios Florida resort is all about the movies, and one of the most successful films of recent years was *Jurassic*

119

Park—which ironically enough was about a theme park. Of course, the moneymaking Spielberg-Creighton extravaganza was also about dinosaurs, and visitors will find plenty of the animatronic variety at Universal's *Jurassic Park* attraction. If not terribly informative, the show certainly stirs up the imagination. For those really into fantasy—such as families with small children—there is also a Barney attraction. Maybe there were once purple dinosaurs, but if so, they were not likely soft and cuddly like Barney. But who cares? Have fun everybody!

Universal Studios Florida
1000 Universal Studio Plaza
Orlando, FL 32819
(407) 363-8000
www.usfinfo.com

Walt Disney World

Disney is famous for animatronic creatures, most of them delightfully fanciful. At the Walt Disney World Epcot Center, however, this technique is used to evoke the world as it was millions of years ago when the earth's fossil energy resources were being created. This vision includes dinosaurs, and naturally, they are the stars of the show. Unlike the other, more fictional attractions at Walt Disney World where one can hope to shake hands with Mickey Mouse, those at the Epcot Center lean toward the scientific and technological.

Walt Disney World
P.O. Box 10040
Lake Buena Vista, FL 32830
(407) 824-4321
www.disney.com

GEORGIA

Fernbank Museum of Natural History

It may not be a *T-rex,* but the twenty-foot tall *Albertosaurus* dominating the Dinosaur Room here at the Fernbank Museum is plenty big enough to impress. Nearly as impressive are the other dinosaur models and fossils that fill the room. The Fernbank is an excellent resource for anyone interested in natural history or on the trail of dinosaurs.

> Fernbank Museum of Natural History
> 707 Clifton Road NE
> Atlanta, GA 30307
> (404) 378-0127
> **www.fernbank.edu**

Fernbank Science Center

Intended primarily as a learning resource for Atlanta area students, the Fernbank Science Center offers a garden, a greenhouse, a planetarium, and a 9,000-square-foot exhibit hall. The latter features a number of captivating dioramas and fossil displays sure to send young imaginations spinning back millions of years to the Age of Dinosaurs. Outstanding among the displays are a *T-rex* skull and a model of *Struthiomimus*. Kids enjoy trying to pronounce the name of the ostrichlike *Struthiomimus*.

> Fernbank Science Center
> 156 Heaton Park Drive
> Atlanta, GA 30307
> (404) 378-4311
> **www.fsc.fernbank.edu**

Georgia Southern University Museum

About the time *Tyrannosaurus rex* raged and roared across the Cretaceous countryside more than sixty-five million years ago, an equally fierce predator roamed the primordial seas. Known as *Mosasaurus*, it had large flippers and rows of vicious teeth good for crushing and tearing apart its prey. Anyone who wants to inspect this monster should try Georgia Southern University in Statesboro where an especially fine mounted *Mosasaurus* skeleton reaches an impressive length of twenty-six feet—about the size of the fictional shark in the movie *Jaws*. In addition to the *Mosasaurus*, the Georgia Southern Museum has on display a forty-million-year-old whale, the lower jaw of a *Tyrannosaurus rex*, and many Pliocene (postdinosaur) fossils found near Statesboro in southeastern Georgia. The latter region was under water during most of the dinosaur era.

> Georgia Southern University Museum
> U.S. 301
> Statesboro, GA 30485
> (912) 681-5444
> www.gasou.edu

Lanier Museum of Natural History

Located on the road to Lake Lanier, this small but delightful museum offers a few dinosaur-related holdings. Mostly they are fossils drawn from the extremely old North Georgia mountains. Also of interest is a large mammoth tusk.

> Lanier Museum of Natural History
> 2601 Buford Dam Road
> Buford, GA 30518
> (770) 932-4460

Macon Museum of Arts and Sciences

This fine community arts and sciences complex started out as a youth museum about half a century ago. Over the years it has grown into an extensive facility featuring an art gallery, science exhibition hall, planetarium, and community theater. Displays include some excellent marine fossils as well as an eighteen-foot model of a prehistoric whale known as *Zygorhiza*—its nickname is "Ziggy."

Many years ago, the staff of what was then the Macon Youth Museum assisted me in my own elementary school–age searches for information on dinosaurs and other prehistoric creatures. A museum-sponsored expedition to a local kaolin mine yielded a number of trilobites and shark teeth, which I still prize. Incidentally, at that time, the museum's mascot was not a whale, but rather a gray squirrel named Newby. A six-foot-tall statue of Newby was kept near the museum entrance. Local children were known to ask whether there were squirrels that large during the Age of Dinosaurs. Apparently not.

Macon Museum of Arts and Sciences
4182 Forsyth Road
Macon, GA 31210
(912) 477-3232
www.masmacon.com

Rock Eagle Museum of Natural History

The Rock Eagle Center is used as a retreat by Georgia 4-H Clubs and various community organizations. A first-rate attraction in its own right, Rock Eagle's delightful Museum of Natural History is well endowed with dinosaurs and other prehistoric creatures. Center visitors are greeted by a sixteen-foot long sea monster—a

Mosasaurus—while elsewhere in the museum they'll encounter three sauropod heads, an *Albertosaurus* mother protecting her hatchlings, and a Carboniferous diorama along with many other fossils, casts, and samples of petrified wood.

The Center also holds fascination for those interested in cultural prehistory. On the grounds is a one hundred-foot-wide effigy of piled stone depicting an eagle. The Rock Eagle complex takes its name from the effigy, which dates back several thousand years. Apparently, the ancient stone mound and another like it about fifteen miles away played an important role in the religious life of the people who lived here nearly 5,000 years ago—at about the same time the pyramids were being built in Egypt.

Rock Eagle Museum of Natural History
350 Rock Eagle Road NW
Eatonton, GA 31024
(706) 484-2800
www.eatonton.com/eagle.html

Weinman Mineral Museum

Excellent geology exhibits and fossils, many of them drawn from the very old North Georgia Mountains and lofty Cumberland Plateau, help visitors retrace the turbulent natural history of the region. Of special interest are fossils retrieved from the Georgia fall line where commercially valuable kaolin deposits are found. The fall line marked the farthest northwestward advance of the oceans during a period of high sea levels more than eighty million years ago. The bright white kaolin, used as a coating for fine paper, consists of the decayed remains of sharks and other sea creatures. Found in and around the kaolin are shark teeth, trilobites, and many other fossil remains from the primordial oceans.

Weinman Mineral Museum
51 Mineral Museum Drive
White, GA 30184
(770) 386-0576
www.chara.gsu.edu

KENTUCKY

Behringer-Crawford Museum

Located in Covington, on the Kentucky side of the Ohio River just south of Cincinnati, the Behringer-Crawford Museum provides interpretive programs associated with nearby Big Bone Lick State Park. On display are many of the best finds excavated from the park. Otherwise, the museum concentrates on northern Kentucky's cultural history and heritage.

Behringer-Crawford Museum
P.O. Box 67
Devou Park/1600 Montague Avenue
Covington, KY 41011
(606) 491-4003

Big Bone Lick State Park

In the northern nub of Kentucky not far from the Ohio River is a place called Big Bone Lick. Pioneers gave it this odd name because of the many unidentified bones or fossils they found here and the natural salt or mineral deposits that attracted animals to the area. The bones were left here from twelve thousand to twenty thousand years ago when Big Bone Lick was a swamp created by an ancient sulfur spring. Many animals such as the mammoth, mastodon, bison, and ground sloth were attracted to the spring and some became ensnared in the

125

sticky quagmire surrounding it. The fossilized remains of these creatures provide a glimpse of life toward the end of the last Ice Age.

Big Bone Lick is now a unique state park offering both indoor and outdoor displays and a small herd of bison or American buffalo. A modest museum features some interesting fossils and interpretive exhibits. Beyond the museum is a one-mile trail providing a view of the buffalo herd and sulfur spring. The park is made all the more delightful by life-size models of mastodon and bison. Sorry, no dinosaurs, but the huge, elephant-like mastodon is sure to impress.

> Big Bone Lick State Park
> 3380 Beaver Road
> Union, KY 41091
> (606) 384-3522
> www.state.ky.us/agencies/parks/bigbone.htm

Blue Licks Battlefield State Park

The salt spring at Blue Licks attracted Indians and frontiersmen the likes of Daniel Boone. But long before these early Americans brought their cattle and horses to drink here, mammoths and other prehistoric animals came here to take advantage of the mineral spring. The bones of some of these Ice Age creatures are on display at the park museum. Boone and his Kentuckians are said to have fought a sharp engagement here with British troops during the Revolutionary War.

> Blue Licks Battlefield State Park
> P.O. Box 66
> Mount Olivet, KY 41064
> (606) 289-5507
> www.state.ky.us/agencies/parks/bluelick.htm

Lexington Children's Museum

This museum is a great place for kids interested in prehistory. Not only are there fascinating fossil exhibits and plenty of dinosaur stuff, but kids are allowed to become young paleontologists and do their own digging. Museum staff help the kids identify their finds. Like many children's museums, this one emphasizes hands-on activities.

Lexington Children's Museum
401 West Short Street
Lexington, KY 40507
(606) 258-3253
www.lexinfo.com/museum/children.html

Northeastern Kentucky History Museum

The state of Kentucky is rich in fossils, and they often find their way into museums dedicated to other subjects. This is the case at the Northeastern Kentucky History Museum in Cedar Cove. Although most of the museum's space is devoted to Kentucky culture and history, it does offer a small, but interesting collection of fossils.

Northeastern Kentucky History Museum
Route 182
Carter Caves, KY 41164
(606) 286-6012
www.state.ky.us/tour/eastern/carterca.htm

LOUISIANA

Audubon Institute

The renowned New Orleans Audubon Institute maintains a major complex of life and natural history related attractions.

These include the famed Audubon Zoo, an aquarium, a nature center, an Imax Theater, and a 30,000-square-foot science center. Still under development, the science center opens exhibitions to the public as they are completed. For information on what is currently available, check the Audubon's delightful Web site.

> Audubon Institute
> 6500 Magazine Street
> New Orleans, LA 70118
> (504) 861-2537
> www.audubonins

Lafayette Museum of Natural History

Lafayette is located well to the west of New Orleans in the heart of Cajun Country. Much of this part of Louisiana is a never-never land only recently emerged from the sea. It consists primarily of marshes and prairies reclaimed from the Gulf with soils dumped here by the Mississippi River over the last few million years. From New Orleans, Lafayette can be reached via Interstate 10, but the route via U.S. 90 takes you through the Atchafalaya Basin, a hundred-mile stretch of semi-land that looks for all the world like those museum murals you see depicting the earth during Cretaceous or Jurassic times. It is very easy to imagine an *Apatosaurus* lumbering through these swamps. Seeing this extraordinary landscape is one very good reason to visit the Lafayette Museum of Natural History. Once you get to the museum you'll find an impressive array of fossils, models, and displays to help you put what you've seen in proper perspective.

> Lafayette Museum of Natural History
> 637 Gerard Park Drive
> Lafayette, LA 70503
> (318) 291-5544
> www.lnhm.org

MISSISSIPPI

Delta State University Museum of Natural History

Since it languished at the bottom of the sea for hundreds of millions of years, Mississippi is not dinosaur country. Naturally enough, most of the fossils found here are of the marine variety, although the remains of Ice Age mammals such as mastodons do turn up. The fossils on exhibit at Delta State University's small but fascinating Museum of Natural History mostly reflect the state's watery past. Fossils of marine turtles, lizards, and early whales are on display.

Keep in mind that paleontology involves the study of life processes and evolution that is still going on today. Delta State maintains an excellent field facility where present-day nature can be studied and appreciated firsthand. The university's Crow's Neck Environmental Education Center in Tishomingo County offers a 530-acre slice of nature crisscrossed with trails and including a laboratory, library, and theater.

> Delta State University Museum of Natural History
> P.O. Box 3262
> Cleveland, MS 38733
> (601) 846-3000
> www.deltast.edu

Mississippi Museum of Natural Science

Jackson's Museum of Natural Science emphasizes the nature and wildlife of the modern world, so dinosaurs are not the big thing here. There are fossils on display, but most of them reflect the state's marine prehistory. An early whalelike ocean predator called a *Zygorhiza* hangs from the ceiling.

129

Mississippi Museum of Natural Science
111 North Jefferson Street
Jackson, MS 39202
(601) 354-7303
www.mdwfp.state.ms.us/museum

Mississippi Petrified Forest

The fifty-million-year-old petrified trees you'll see here won't quite take you back to the era of the dinosaurs—it ended sixty-five million years ago. Nonetheless, this unusual paleontological find provides a helpful illustration of how natural chemical processes turn living matter into fossil.

Mississippi Petrified Forest
124 Forest Park Road
P.O. Box 37
Flora, MS 39071
(601) 879-8189
www.mspetrifiedforest.com

Mississippi State University/Dunn-Seiler Museum

Located on the campus of Mississippi State University in Starkville is the Dunn-Seiler Museum, a good place to see some prehistoric fossils. Here you'll find a *Triceratops* skull, fossils of the phytosaur—a Triassic crocodile-like meat-eater, a saber-toothed cat skeleton, and much more.

Mississippi State University/Dunn-Seiler Museum
Department of Geosciences
P.O. Box 5448
Mississippi State University, MS 39762
www.msstate.edu

NORTH CAROLINA

Aurora Fossil Museum

The geology and paleo-history of the Carolina coastal plain provide the emphasis for this fossil museum in Aurora. Since oceans washed this region throughout much of prehistory, most of what you'll see here are marine fossils such as shark teeth, whale bone, shells, and coral. Many of the fossils were taken from local phosphate mines. Visitors are allowed to sort through tailings from the mines and keep any fossils they find. The museum serves as headquarters for the Aurora Fossil Club, a selective group that maintains a membership list of only fifty. You may contact the club at the address below.

> Aurora Fossil Museum
> 400 Main Street
> P.O. Box 352
> Aurora, NC 27806
> (252) 322-4238

Discovery Place

Charlotte's Discovery Place has become one of the South's major attractions, and it is easy to see why. Staff members describe their 140,000-square-foot educational facility as a "hands-on, minds-on museum," and the emphasis is definitely on youthful exploration. Apparently, the "touch first and ask questions later" philosophy of Discovery Place works very well since more than 700,000 visitors pass through its doors each year. Nearly a quarter-million of the museum's patrons are schoolchildren.

Inside the museum visitors find a bewildering array of offerings such as a tropical rain forest, wave tank and aquarium, space science center, five-story Omnimax theater, and amateur radio room. But dino-hunters—and practically everyone else under the age of one hundred—will head straight for the robotic dinosaurs. They move, they menace, and they roar, much as scientists think the originals did more than sixty-five million years ago. Meticulously crafted in one-quarter to full size, these lively dinos are driven by compressed air. Among them are the *Dimetrodon*—a pre-dinosaur reptile—*Stegosaurus*, with its bony plates, *Apatosaurus*, with its long, snaky neck, *Triceratops*, with its forty-inch horns, *Pachycephalosaurus*, with its thick skull, and everybody's favorite, the *Tyrannosaurus*, with its big bite.

Discovery Place
301 North Tryon Street
Charlotte, NC 28202
(704) 372-6261
www.discoveryplace.org

Greensboro Natural Science Center

In the Dinosaur gallery at the Greensboro Natural Science Center, visitors come face-to-face with a toothy, thirty-six-foot model of *Tyrannosaurus rex*. There are other models and plenty of fossils in the gallery as well. Elsewhere, the museum offers a gem and mineral gallery, petting zoo, and planetarium. The museum store is called the Thesaurus (a rather delightful pun) Shop. There you'll find rocks, minerals, dinosaur models, and real fossils.

Greensboro Natural Science Center
4301 Lawndale Drive
Greensboro, NC 27455
(336) 288-3769
www.greensboro.com/sciencecenter

*T*HIS WAS *no dinosaur, but rather an early reptile that may very well have been an ancestor of the mammals. The four-footed, lizardlike* Dimetrodon *had a large sail on its back, likely used for regulating its body temperature. By turning the broad side of the sail to the sun, the animal might have warmed its body quickly. It is thought by some that this adaptation may have been an early link in the chain of evolution that led to warm-bloodedness in mammals. The ten-foot-long* Dimetrodon *lived during the Permian period long before the beginning of the Age of Dinosaurs and was likely a meat-eater.*

DIMETRODON

North Carolina Museum of Life and Science

North Carolina has several fine nature museums, and this is among the best. Its state-of-the-art exhibits are designed to be hands-on and highly interactive. Visitors may examine a full-size model of NASA's lunar lander, touch an artificial tornado, or take a walk through the earth's 4.5-billion-year prehistory. A feature of special interest to dino-hunters is the outdoor Prehistory Trail with its dinosaur models. The museum also has on display an array of interesting fossil materials including a cast of a *Tyrannosaurus* skull. Especially attractive to children are the museum's live animal exhibits, such as the "Meet the Muskrat" display.

North Carolina Museum of Life and Science
433 Murray Avenue
Durham, NC 27704
(919) 220-5429
www.ils.unc.edu/NCMLS/ncmls.html

North Carolina Museum of Natural Science

The North Carolina equivalent of the Smithsonian Institution is the Museum of Natural Science in Raleigh. With more than a million specimens in its collections, the museum thoroughly documents the wildlife, botany, geology, and prehistory of the state. With the recent opening of its new, multilevel complex in downtown Raleigh, the museum has become one of the premier natural science facilities in the nation.

The first floor celebrates some of North Carolina's best-known natural treasures, for instance: two thousand-year-old trees, the world's oldest mountains (the Appalachians) and second-oldest river (the New), and the highest peak east of the Mississippi (the 6,684-foot Mount Mitchell). Also on the first floor are a coastal exhibition with dioramas, whale skeletons, and other displays celebrating the state's dynamic sea coast.

The second and third floors are largely devoted to the breathtaking "Mountains to the Sea" exhibition, which takes visitors from the summit of the high Appalachians, through the Piedmont, and across the coastal plain to the Atlantic. The third-floor portion of this exhibition is where you'll find dinosaurs. Here fossils and dioramas provide a glimpse at the state's prehistory. Fossils and replicas of *Tyrannosaurus rex*, *Triceratops*, and other prehistoric vertebrates provide the highlights. Climbing above the dinos to the fourth floor, you'll find butterflies and the like. There is also a lovely rooftop cafe.

Housed in this fine, new facility is the vast collection of specimens brought over from the old museum. Among these are 800,000 fishes, 100,000 amphibians and reptiles, 7,800 mammals, 18,000 birds, and more than 100,000 fossils.

> North Carolina Museum of Natural Science
> 102 North Salisbury Street
> Raleigh, NC 27603
> (910) 733-7450
> www.naturalsciences.org/stone.htm

Schiele Museum of Natural History

The Schiele takes visitors on a walk through time allowing them to follow the evolution of life on the earth. Fossils and dioramas retrace the development of single-cell and multi-cell forms, the emergence of the first amphibians from the sea, and the appearance of far more complex creatures such as dinosaurs.

> Schiele Museum of Natural History
> 1500 East Garrison Boulevard
> Gastonia, NC 28054
> (704) 866-6900
> www.schielemuseum.org

SOUTH CAROLINA

Charleston Museum

This treasury of old and interesting stuff should be explored, if for no other reason, because this was the first museum in the United States. In fact, it was founded in 1773, before there was a United States. Among its key attractions is a full-size replica of a Confederate submarine—that's right, a Civil War submersible, the CSS *Hunley*. There are also clothing, photographs, table silver, games, vehicles, and a wealth of other objects documenting the history of South Carolina and the graceful city of Charleston. The museum's fossil holdings consist primarily of Cenozoic birds, mammals, and marine life. Whales are well represented in the collection.

Charleston Museum
360 Meeting Street
Charleston, SC 29403
(843) 722-2996
www.charlestonmuseum.com

South Carolina State Museum

South Carolina's State Museum in Columbia has a separate Natural History Division with strong collections on vertebrate paleontology and entomology. Naturally, the focus here is on South Carolina prehistory, and much of what you'll see is from the Cenozoic period. There are very interesting exhibits on how fossils are formed and what we learn from them. In the Pleistocene Hall are skeletons or models of a mastodon, giant beaver, and glyptodont.

South Carolina State Museum
301 Gervais Street
Columbia, SC 29201
(803) 898-4921
www.museum.state.sc.us

TENNESSEE

Coon Creek Science Center

Some seventy million years ago, the Gulf of Mexico extended right up into the heart of what is now the United States. At that time, much of west Tennessee was underwater and teeming with marine life. The remains of sea creatures can now be seen in Upper Cretaceous rocks found throughout the region. One particularly rich fossil cache is located on Coon Creek in rural McNairy County. The fossil beds here are part of the Coon Creek Science Center, a facility used mostly by public school students who take part in "fossil camps" and learn how to find, identify, and properly handle fossils. The facility is open to the public only on an advance-reservation basis.

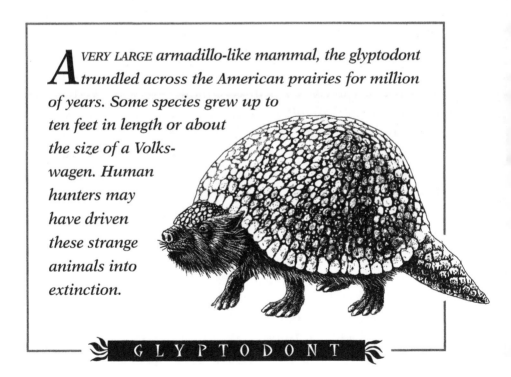

A VERY LARGE armadillo-like mammal, the glyptodont trundled across the American prairies for million of years. Some species grew up to ten feet in length or about the size of a Volkswagen. Human hunters may have driven these strange animals into extinction.

GLYPTODONT

Coon Creek Science Center
Memphis Museums
3050 Central Avenue
Memphis, TN 38111
(901) 320-6320
www.memphismuseums.org

McClung Museum of Natural History

A general-interest museum with collections in anthropology, archaeology, decorative arts, and local history, as well as natural history, the McClung is a broad-based facility. Part of the University of Tennessee Knoxville, the museum is housed in a forty thousand-square-foot building with about a quarter of that area used for exhibits.

Geology and fossil holdings at the McClung concentrate on materials found in the state of Tennessee. Included are fossils of a duck-billed *Hadrosaurus*, the only dinosaur bones ever found in Tennessee. There are also skulls and fossils of Ice Age mammals such as mastodons, giant sloths, dire wolves, giant beavers, and saber-toothed cats. Fossilized crinoids (marine invertebrates that lived about 350 million years ago) are common in east Tennessee and well represented at the museum.

A special attraction at the McClung is its small but fascinating exhibit on "Lucy," the three-million-year-old hominid found in East Africa about twenty-five years ago. The exhibit traces the evolution of humans with fossil casts, stone tools, and various interpretive aids.

McClung Museum of Natural History
1327 Circle Park Drive
University of Tennessee
Knoxville, TN 37996
(423) 974-2144
mcclungmuseum.utk.edu

Memphis Pink Palace Museum

Part of an educational complex including a planetarium, Imax theater, and (at separate locations) a nature center and a pair of historic homes, the playfully named Pink Palace Museum offers one of Tennessee's best prehistory exhibits. Since West Tennessee was underwater during much of the Age of Dinosaurs, fossil displays here tend to emphasize marine life. However, there is a life-size model of *Dilophosaurus*, the crested Jurassic meat-eater. Also on hand are a mounted mosasaur and mastodon, and some interesting dinosaur trackways.

Memphis Pink Palace Museum
3050 Central Avenue
Memphis, TN 38111
(901) 320-6320
www.memphismuseums.org

VIRGINIA

Culpeper Museum of History

The author once lived in Culpeper, a quaint Virginia town surrounded by lovely rolling hills and bucolic farming country. The place is far less well known for prehistory than it is for the Civil War history—an important cavalry battle was fought nearby. As a matter of fact, Robert E. Lee, J. E. B. Stuart, Ulysses S. Grant, and even Abraham Lincoln all came here at one time or another. So, too, did countless dinosaurs—but many millions of years earlier. Trackways and other sure signs of these Mesozoic visits have been unearthed by local stone quarrying operations. The Culpeper Museum in the middle of town contains a few of these fossils. There you'll also see relics of what is known in Culpeper as "The War Between the States."

Culpeper Museum of History
Locust Street
Culpeper, VA 22701
(540) 829-1749

Virginia Living Museum

A combination planetarium, nature center, aquarium, and zoo, the Virginia Living Museum in Newport News offers a broad view of science. In the James River Geology Hall you'll see an *Allosaurus* skull and a variety of dinosaur fossils, casts, and trackways. Cenozoic exhibits include a giant shark tooth, a mastodon tooth, and a skull cast of a saber-toothed cat. A

*L*IKE AN *armored car on legs, the six thousand-pound* Euoplocephalus *had thick, bony plates and rows of sharp spikes along its back to protect it from predators. Should its armor fail to discourage some especially tenacious enemy, this plant-eater could fight back, wielding its heavy tail like a club. The* Euoplocephalus *was a Late Cretaceous relative of the similarly built* Ankylosaurus.

EUOPLOCEPHALUS

140

locally gathered fossil shell collection dates back from three to five million years. Not far from the prehistory exhibits are real live deer, raccoons, and turkeys.

Virginia Living Museum
524 J. Clyde Morris Boulevard
Newport News, VA 23601
(757) 595-1900
www.valivingmuseum.org

Virginia Museum of Natural History

Among the permanent exhibitions at the Virginia Museum of Natural History in Martinsville is a series of displays on "The Age of Reptiles." Included are casts of fossils and trackways, most of them from Virginia. Also on exhibit are prehistoric insects—some of the oldest found on this continent—extinct mammals, and a marvelous selection of rocks and minerals. The museum Web site is excellent and has its own separate Dinosaur Gallery featuring *Allosaurus*, *Apatosaurus*, *Parasaurolophus*, and *Euoplocephalus*.

Virginia Museum of Natural History
1001 Douglas Avenue
Martinsville, VA 24112
(540) 666-8600
www.vmnh.org

WEST VIRGINIA

Bluestone Museum

Located in the historic town of Hinton, West Virginia, the Bluestone Museum shows off a small collection of rocks and fossils, most of them collected locally in the New River Gorge. The

141

ironically named New River is itself something of a living fossil since it is believed to be among the oldest rivers on the planet. The New actually predates the dinosaurs. Incidentally, Hinton is John Henry country, and there is a museum here devoted to him and the rich railroad tradition of this mountainous state.

Bluestone Museum
Route 87 Box 10
Hinton, WV 25951
(304) 466-1454

West Virginia State Museum

Dino-hunters who also appreciate quilts, antiques, and the like will feel right at home at this museum in the Cultural Complex at Charleston, the state capital. While West Virginia is mountainous nowadays, it was covered by the sea throughout much of prehistory. As a result, you'll mostly see marine fossils here.

West Virginia State Museum
Division of Culture and History
Cultural Center
1900 Kawawha Boulevard
Charleston, WV 25305
(304) 558-0220
www.wvnet.edu

Dinos in
the Midwest

Aurora Historical Museum

In 1934, government construction workers uncovered what they believed to be a cache of cattle bones left by early pioneers. In fact, they had stumbled across the remains of a long-extinct mastodon. The bones are now on display at a modest but interesting historical museum in the town of Aurora, west of Chicago.

Aurora Historical Museum
317 Cedar Street
Aurora, IL 60506
(630) 897-9029

Chicago Academy of Science

Founded in 1857, the Academy of Sciences is Chicago's oldest scientific organization and dates to well before the time dinosaurs became a subject of serious research in the United States. Its original purpose was the study of Illinois flora and fauna, a pursuit Academy members took up with enthusiasm. By 1865, they had gathered so many specimens that a large museum was built to house them all. Alas, the building was destroyed along with its huge collection during the great Chicago Fire in 1871. Afterward, the well-known and well-loved Academy museum on North Clark Street was completed in 1893.

Dedicated to increasing public understanding and appreciation of science and nature, the Academy is both a research and an educational institution. It has long played a prominent role in many fields of scientific endeavor, including paleontology. Dino-hunters who visit the museum won't be disappointed. Games and interactive displays add considerable impact to the fossil exhibits. The Academy holds about 30,000 fossils, which represent a relatively small percentage of its overall collection of 230,000 specimens.

> Chicago Academy of Science
> 2060 North Clark Street
> Chicago, IL 60614
> (773) 871-2668
> **www.chias.org**

Elgin Public Museum

Among the fifteen thousand specimens and artifacts to be found in this small museum are a number of dinosaur fossils and other interesting prehistoric materials. The city of Elgin and its museum are located west of Chicago.

> Elgin Public Museum
> 225 Grand Boulevard
> Elgin, IL 60120
> (847) 741-6655

Fryxell Geology Museum

The remarkable Fryxell Museum at Augustana College contains an astounding array of fossils. Some date all the way back to the early days of life on our planet. Dinosaur displays include *Tyrannosaurus*, *Allosaurus*, and *Triceratops* skulls and a wide variety of other fossils. But the strength of this collection lies in its breadth. It ranges from the early living cells that appeared in the oceans billions of years ago to extinct camels and saber-toothed cats from the Ice Age.

Students at Augustana may take advantage of outdoor field courses in geology and paleontology. Classes travel to the badlands of northwest Nebraska to collect fossils and conduct on-site research.

> Fryxell Geology Museum
> Swenson Science Building
> Augustana College
> Rock Island, IL 61201
> (309) 794-7000
> **www.augustana.edu/geology/museum.htm**

Illinois State Museum

Among the 200,000 specimens in the extensive geology holdings here is a strong collection of carboniferous fossils. Most of the museum's vertebrate fossils are of Pliocene (Late Cenozoic) mammals. While dinosaurs are not the prime focus here, there are many fascinating exhibits including one on the impact of the Ice Ages on the Midwest. Of particular interest is the museum's fine on-line exhibit. You can access it at the Web address below.

> Illinois State Museum
> Spring and Edward Streets
> Springfield, IL 62706
> (217) 782-7386
> **www.museum.state.il.us**

Western Illinois University Geology Museum

This museum is devoted to geology rather than paleontology, but keep in mind that the two disciplines are close kin. The university geology department maintains a fine museum containing extensive collections of minerals and many fossils. The paleontology displays feature the egg-filled nest of a *Protoceratops*. This Late Cretaceous plant-eater had an armored head and a snout resembling a bird's beak. No monster, it ranged up to about six feet in length.

> Western Illinois University Geology Museum
> 115 Tillman Hall
> Macomb, IL 61455
> (309) 298-1151
> www.ECNet.NET/users/migeol

INDIANA

Children's Museum of Indianapolis

Indianapolis can boast one of the most attractive and kid-friendly children's museums in the United States. Outside, young folks are greeted by a full-size *Tyrannosaurus* model. If this toothy guardian were the real thing, he would likely gobble up the wide-eyed children who stand and stare at him, but he's harmless. The fossil collection inside the museum is relatively small but adequate to its task of getting young folks interested in paleontology. There are several articulated dinosaur skeletons and a mounted mastodon. Incidentally, this is one of the largest children's museums in the world, and paleontology is only one of many fields of study that can be explored here.

A NUMBER OF beaked and horned dinosaurs appear during the Cretaceous. Among the first of these rhinoceros-like creatures was the Protoceratops, *a relatively small, four-legged plant-eater. Unlike the* Triceratops, *the* Protoceratops *had very modest horns consisting of a pair of bony ridges above the eyes. Since its hind quarters were longer and more powerfully built than its forelimbs, some paleontologists think it might have risen onto two legs on occasion. Perhaps it did so to snip at juicy plants otherwise just out of its reach. The* Protoceratops *is of particular importance historically, since one of its fossilized nests— uncovered during the 1920s, contained the first dinosaur eggs ever discovered.*

PROTOCERATOPS

In addition to the many attractions at the exhibit hall, the museum maintains a number of excellent on-line exhibits including a particularly attractive series of paleontology pages where browsers will find colorfully illustrated descriptions of more than two dozen types of dinosaurs.

Children's Museum of Indianapolis
3000 North Meridian Street
Indianapolis, IN 46208
(317) 924-5431
www.childrensmuseum.org

Falls of the Ohio State Park

For many millions of years, this part of the Midwest was covered by a shallow sea teaming with life. In time, thick fossil beds accumulated on the sea floor. Today, near New Albany, Indiana, these marine fossils lie exposed in layers dating back almost four hundred million years. Visitors to Falls of the Ohio Sate Park are encouraged to explore these remains and discover Ohio's prehistory for themselves. To protect this rich paleontological resource, fossil collecting is prohibited, but there is much to be learned here. Keep in mind that most of what you'll see dates to Devonian times long before the appearance of the dinosaurs.

Falls of the Ohio State Park
206 West Riverside Drive
Clarksville, IN 47129
(812) 280-9970
www.cismall.com/fallsoftheohio

Fort Wayne Geology Museum/Purdue University

Dinosaurs are not on center stage here. However, the museum features displays of Ice Age mammals and maintains an ample collection of fossils. Geology museums such as this one at Purdue provide an excellent background for dino-hunters since geology and paleontology are closely related fields.

Fort Wayne Geology Museum/Purdue University
2101 Coliseum Boulevard East
Fort Wayne, IN 46805
(219) 481-6100

Indiana State Museum

In south-central Indiana is a mysterious underground chamber known as Megenity Cave. Over a period of perhaps 100,000 years animals vanished into its dark subterranean recesses, became trapped, and were never seen in the light again. The remains of these unfortunate creatures—dire wolves, tapirs, armadillos, and many other species—now form the bulk of an extensive fossil collection at the Indiana State Museum in Indianapolis. The museum also maintains collections of verte-brate and invertebrate fossils found elsewhere in Indiana, but has little in the way of dinosaur materials.

> Indiana State Museum
> 202 North Alabama Street
> Indianapolis, IN 46204
> (317) 232-1637
> www.state.in.us/ism/museum/paleontology

Joseph Moore Museum of Natural History

In 1852 young Joseph Moore came to Earlman College to teach science. In all, this midwestern "Mr. Chips" would devote more

A VERY LARGE *early wolf, this animal grew to more than six feet in length and hunted Ice Age plains and hills throughout North America. The Dire Wolf is the ancestor of modern dogs and other modern dog-like species such as coyotes.*

DIRE WOLF

DINOS IN THE MIDWEST

than fifty years of his life to the institution and its students, eventually serving as president and later as curator of the college museum. A man of catholic interests, Moore filled the museum with an astounding array of specimens and artifacts he helped gather from all over the planet. Today, the museum is named for him, and it still reflects his indefatigable curiosity and fascination with the world around him. Included in its collections are more than 60 mounted big-game trophies from Africa and the American West, nearly 26,000 mounted insects, and as many as 10,000 ornithological and mammalian specimens. Dino-hunters will take particular interest in the museum's *Allosaurus* and its wide array of fossils. Among them is a giant Pleistocene beaver, one of only a few items saved from a fire that gutted the old museum about seventy years ago. In addition to the singed beaver, visitors who look around a bit will also find a giant sloth, a mastodon, and yes, even an Egyptian mummy. Somewhat like the attic of an eccentric old professor, the museum has a little of everything.

Joseph Moore Museum of Natural History
Earlham College
National Road West
Richmond, IN 47374
(765) 983-1303
www.earlham.edu

IOWA

Iowa Historical Museum

If the *Tyrannosaurus rex* and other meat-eating giants of the dinosaur era are a little too scary, you might try this Des Moines, Iowa, museum where the most important fossil collections are those of crinoids. These sea lily-like marine animals are definitely not the stuff of Steven Spielberg movies.

Nonetheless, serious students of paleontology take them quite seriously as they dominated the earth's vast oceans for more millions of years than are worth counting. Crinoid lovers may also want to try out the Web site listed below.

Iowa Historical Museum
600 East Locust Street
Des Moines, IA 50319
(515) 281-5111
www.state.ia.us

Madison County Crinoid Collection

The stupendously popular novel and Clint Eastwood movie *The Bridges of Madison County* helped put little Winterset on the map. But to fossil fanatics and fans of crinoids or other prehistoric marine invertebrates, Madison County was already notable. The county's historical museum houses the collection of the renowned crinoid expert Amel Priest. Incidentally, there really are some lovely covered bridges in this bucolic Iowa county. What is more, Winterset is the birthplace of a man named Marion Morrison. You might know him better as screen star and king of the westerns John (the Duke) Wayne.

Madison County Crinoid Collection
815 South Second Avenue
Winterset, IA 50273
(515) 462-2134
www.madisoncounty.com

University of Iowa Museum of Natural History

When dinosaurs walked the earth, they did their walking in places other than Iowa. This part of the Midwest was underwater during nearly all of the Age of Dinosaurs. That's why the local fossil collections at the University of Iowa Museum of Natural History are a bit thin on dinosaur material. However, they are rich in marine invertebrates. The museum features displays on Ice Age mammals along with marine fossils dating back to the Devonian period more than 350 million years ago.

A short distance from Iowa City, home of the university and its natural history museum, is the Coralville Dam. The great midwestern floods of 1993 severely eroded the dam's spillway, exposing a bank of Devonian fossils. Since then, the spillway has become a popular hiking destination for fossil buffs.

> University of Iowa Museum of Natural History
> 10 McBride Hall
> Iowa City, IA 52242
> (319) 335-0480
> www.cgrer.edu/iowa_environment/museum/Museum.html

KANSAS

Fick Fossil Museum

One wonders what sort of bait an angler would need to haul in a fifteen-foot fish like the one on display at the Fick. Monsters like that are caught only in stories told by Kansas fishermen, since these big fish have been extinct since Cretaceous times when an ocean covered the state. Not surprisingly, most of the fossils discovered in Kansas are those of sea creatures, and the same is true of most fossils found at the Fick. In addition to its large fossil collection, the Fick offers displays of branding irons, wildflowers, wood carvings, and many other fascinating things.

> Fick Fossil Museum
> 700 West Third
> Oakley, KS 67748
> (785) 672-4839
> www.oakley-kansas.com/fick.html

Johnston Geology Museum

This excellent geology museum is named for Dr. Paul Johnston, who taught earth sciences to Emporia students for more than thirty-eight years. Dr. Johnson helped found the museum and also served as its curator for many years. Visitors will find an abundance of fossils and other specimens at this museum on the Emporia State University campus. Outstanding among the exhibits are a seventeen-foot Cretaceous mosasaur, an eight-foot mastodon tusk, and a giant ground sloth. The geology displays here are extensive and feature the internationally known Hamilton Quarry collection of marine fossils. You can take a virtual tour of the museum at the Web address listed below.

> Johnston Geology Museum
> Emporia State University
> 200 Commercial Street
> Emporia, KS 66801
> (316) 341-5330
> **www.emporia.edu/earthsci/museum/museum.htm**

McPherson Museum

Ice Age fossils dominate the paleontology collection at the McPherson Museum, so you won't find much in the way of dinosaurs here. Prehistoric mammal displays include a saber-toothed cat, dire wolf, and giant sloth. Much of the museum is devoted to local and regional history.

> McPherson Museum
> 1130 East Euclid
> McPherson, KS 67460
> (316) 241-8464

Pioneer Museum

As its name suggests, the Pioneer Museum in Ashland, Kansas, celebrates those hardy folk who moved onto the Kansas plains during the mid-nineteenth century replacing the Indians and buffalo. Frontier guns, barbed wire, quilts, and the like are prominent among the displays. However, there is also a small fossil collection consisting mostly of Pleistocene mammals and very much older marine invertebrates.

> Pioneer Museum
> 430 West Fourth Street (U.S. 160)
> Ashland, KS 67831
> (316) 635-2227

Sternberg Memorial Museum of Natural History

Once located on the Fort Hays University campus, the famed Sternberg Museum of Natural History now occupies a domed structure beside Interstate 70 across town from the school. This fine, new facility has made room for one of the nation's largest and most spectacular paleontology exhibits—a Cretaceous diorama offering a sweeping view of life on the planet some eighty million years ago. Visitors walk through the diorama, which begins with displays of undersea life. Moving up a ramp, they emerge into a transitional beach zone and then finally onto land where they encounter a small herd of robotic dinosaurs. This impressive diorama is a must-see for dino-hunters who will love the moving *Hadrosaurus* and *Tyrannosaurus rex* models.

The Sternberg has long been known for the breadth and depth of its collections. Among them are over 32,000 pressed plants, 70,000 insects, 6,500 snakes and amphibians, 100,000 fishes, 37,000 mammals, and—get this—more than three million fossil specimens. Fossils from the Cretaceous, when a shallow sea covered much of Kansas, are particularly numerous and scientifically worthy.

Sternberg Memorial Museum of Natural History
3000 Sternberg Drive
Hays, KS 67601
(785) 628-4286
www.fhsu.edu/sternberg

University of Kansas Museum of Natural History

Fossils at the University of Kansas Natural History Museum include fish, birds, mammals, invertebrates, and reptiles as well as dinosaurs. Dino-hunters will be thrilled by the mounted *Pteranodon*, a flying reptile with an airplane-size wingspan of twenty-five feet. There are also *Archaeopteryx* fossils here as well as the remains of large marine reptiles such as plesiosaurs and mosasaurs. Land fossils are less numerous since Kansas was mostly covered by ocean during Cretaceous times. However, there is a *Triceratops* skull on display. Don't miss the impressive "Arctic Panorama," a diorama depicting plants and animals native to the far north. The museum offers a very informative and colorful on-line exhibit, which can be accessed through the Web site address listed below.

University of Kansas Museum of Natural History
Jayhawk Boulevard
Lawrence, KS 66045
(913) 864-4540
www.nhm.ukans.edu

MICHIGAN

Cranbrook Institute of Science

The Cranbrook Institute is dedicated to opening up the world of science for adults and children through its exhibits and outreach programs. Its paleontology, astronomy, and other offerings are especially attractive to kids, and every year more than 100,000 youngsters visit the Bloomfield Hills, Michigan, facility. Among the many interesting things they see are dinosaur tracks and other fossils. Near the entrance is a full-scale model of a *Stegosaurus*. The museum's Ice Age mammal collection is also worth a look. Check with the museum staff for information about special classes on dinosaurs and other science topics.

> Cranbrook Institute of Science
> 1221 North Woodward
> P.O. Box 801
> Bloomfield Hills, MI 48303
> (248) 645-3200
> www.cranbrook.edu

Kalamazoo Museum

You won't find much in the way of dinosaur material here. However, there are some interesting fossils on display as well as a cache of mastodon bones found near Kalamazoo.

> Kalamazoo Museum
> 230 North Rose Street
> Kalamazoo, MI 49007
> (616) 373-7990
> www.kvcc.edu

Kingman Museum of Natural History

Located in Battle Creek, Michigan, the Kingman Museum features a *Protoceratops* skull. There are also dinosaur eggs and many other fossils on display.

Kingman Museum of Natural History
175 Limit Street
Battle Creek, MI 49107
(616) 965-5117

Michigan State University Museum

Founded in 1857, this is one of the oldest university museums in the country. Its holdings and exhibits are especially rich in the field of paleontology, and that, of course, is good news for dino-hunters. The museum has more than four hundred mounted animals on display, including full skeletons of *Allosaurus* and *Stegosaurus*.

The museum has an entire hall devoted to the subject of evolution. It dramatizes the story of life on the planet from its earliest beginnings billions of years ago down to the present day. Visitors to the Hall of Evolution will find the skull of a *Tyrannosaurus rex* and plenty of other dinosaur fossils.

This fine facility has many attractions besides its dinosaurs. Among them are one of the nation's largest mammal collections with more than thirty-four thousand specimens and cultural holdings and displays featuring more than eighty-nine thousand artifacts.

Michigan State University Museum
West Circle Drive
East Lansing, MI 48824
(517) 355-2370
www.museum.cl.msu.edu

University of Michigan Exhibit Museum

The fossil collection at the University of Michigan Museum of Paleontology is a big one. The fourth largest university collection in the United States, it contains more than 200,000 cataloged vertebrate specimens and nearly two million invertebrate specimens. The vertebrate collection emphasizes late Paleozoic amphibians and reptiles and early Cenozoic mammals. The museum also operates a large fossil preparation and casting laboratory.

Not surprisingly, there are plenty of dinosaurs here. Among the exhibits are a mounted *Stegosaurus*, *Allosaurus*, and *Coelophysis* along with many other dino fossils. *T-rex* fans will find a particularly impressive skull of their favorite carnivore.

Don't miss the Exhibit Museum's on-line dioramas, which are accessible through the Internet address listed below.

University of Michigan Exhibit Museum
Paleontology Museum
1109 Geddes Avenue
Ann Arbor, MI 48109
(313) 764-0478
www.exhibits.lsa.umich.edu

MINNESOTA

Science Museum of Minnesota

Saint Paul's noted Science Museum of Minnesota attracts more than a million visitors each year, many of them children, and it is easy to see why. The museum allows its visitors to explore and discover natural and technical worlds around them by means of hands-on exhibits. Here you can run your own tests on Mississippi River water or actually touch a (man-made in this case) tornado.

Dino-hunters will find plenty to interest them at the Paleontology Hall where they will encounter the world's largest mounted *Camptosaurus* skeleton. A plant-eater, the twenty-foot-long *Camptosaurus* was not huge by dinosaur standards. Some may be more impressed by the museum's eighty-foot-long *Diplodocus*, menacing *Allosaurus*, or *Tyrannosaurus* skull.

The Science Museum also offers an Omnitheater, a science theater, and a variety of school, youth, and continuing education programs. Some of the museum's exhibits can be sampled on-line at the Web site listed on the facing page.

CAMPTOSAURUS

A LATE JURASSIC *ornithopod, the* Iguanodon-*like* Camptosaurus *was apparently a very successful and widespread dinosaur since its fossils can be found in many areas. This twenty-foot-long plant-eater may have walked on two legs or four depending on its needs. An unusual characteristic of the creature was its breathing passages, which were structured in such a way that it could breathe easily even while gobbling great mouthfuls of plant material. No doubt, the* Camptosaurus *itself provided food for a variety of hungry carnivores. Fossils of* Camptosaurus *are on display in many American museums.*

Science Museum of Minnesota
30 East 10th Street
Saint Paul, MN 55101
(651) 221-9444
www.sci.mus.mn.us/html

MISSOURI

Mastodon State Park

A popular theory concerning the prehistoric mastodon holds that it was the appearance of humans in North America that led to the extinction of this elephant-like species. A find made near Imperial, Missouri, in 1976 lends some weight to that notion. Here paleontologists unearthed a mastodon skeleton with a stone spearhead lodged in its ribs. At the very least this discovery proved that humans and mastodons shared the continent during the late Ice Age. You'll see a mastodon model at the visitors center and can follow a path to the excavation site.

Mastodon State Park
1551 Seckman Road
Imperial, MO 63052
(314) 464-2976

NEBRASKA

Agate Fossil Beds National Monument

The 3,000 acres of Agate Fossil Beds National Monument were once part of a huge northwestern Nebraska cattle ranch owned by Captain James Cook. A highly productive cattle range, the Agate Springs Ranch eventually proved even more fruitful as a source of Miocene fossils. This is due in part to a mysterious disaster that took place here almost 20 million

161

*T*HE NORTH AMERICAN Moropus *survived for tens of millions of years, in fact, throughout much of the Cenozoic period only to vanish from the fossil record a few million years ago. Whatever made this strange animal so successful must be of little use nowadays, since the modern world contains nothing even remotely like it. The Moropus looked something like a horse, but it had sharp claws much like a bear. Probably the animal used its claws for defense or to manipulate foliage.*

M
O
R
O
P
U
S

years ago. Thousands of animals were trapped and killed by a flood or some similar calamity. Their bones were covered by mud and sand and fossilized to await excavation and study by modern scientists. Since the beds are still under excavation, visitors may very well see paleontologists hard at work here. From the visitors center, a two-mile trail leads to Carnegie Hill and University Hill, both active fossil quarries. Among the countless interesting finds researchers have made in these beds are the fossilized remains of horned mammals such as the horselike *Moropus*.

Agate Fossil Beds National Monument
301 River Road
Harrison, NE 69346
(308) 668-2211
www.nps.gov/agfo

Ashfall Fossil Beds State Historical Park

One day about ten million years ago, herds of rhinoceros, camels, and delicate three-toed horses gathered at a watering hole in what is now Antelope County, Nebraska. Perhaps they were trying to escape the choking ash hurdling toward them from a huge volcanic eruption in faraway Idaho, but they got no farther than the water's edge. The ash buried them, preserving their skeletons just where they fell, still locked in their death poses. Today, the site of this prehistoric disaster serves as a valuable resource for paleontologists.

A two thousand-square-foot protective structure called the Rhino Barn protects an especially productive portion of the fossil quarry. A walkway provides public access to some of the excavations where visitors may very well see paleontologists at work. Skeletons inside the barn are uncovered and displayed exactly as they were found. Seeing these unfortunate creatures, struck down long ago by a calamity they could not have understood or foreseen, is a poignant experience.

The Ashfall Fossil Beds were discovered less than thirty years ago when spring rains cut a gully through a Nebraska cornfield exposing a baby rhino skull. Teams from the Nebraska State Museum and the University of Nebraska eventually enlarged the gully and found the extraordinary trove of fossils now known to exist beneath the field.

Ashfall Fossil Beds State Historical Park
P.O. Box 66
Royal, NE 68773
(402) 893-2000
www.ngpc.state.ne.us/parks/ashfall.html

Fort Robinson State Park/Trailside Museum

One of several fine public museums operated in cooperation with the University of Nebraska, the Trailside Museum in Crawford offers few dinosaur materials. However, there are some excellent Pliocene fossils on display including those of a mammoth.

Fort Robinson is itself an important reminder of the past. The fort was established in 1874 to protect the local Indian agency, and it remained an active military post right up until 1948. Famous Native American tribal leaders such as Crazy Horse and Red Cloud spent time here. The park celebrates the fort's history with stagecoach rides, chuck wagon cookouts, and many other activities that allow visitors to relive Old West experiences. Nature lovers will enjoy the park's twenty-two thousand-acre reserve with its open horizons, trout streams, and buffalo herd.

Fort Robinson State Park/Trailside Museum
Highway 20
Crawford, NE 69339
(308) 665-2900

Nebraska State Museum of Natural History

A tremendous bronze replica of a mammoth stands guard outside the University of Nebraska's Morrill Hall, home of the Nebraska State Museum of Natural History. Known to his admirers as "Archie," the mammoth serves as an appropriate symbol for the museum, which contains one of America's finest paleontology collections and a world-famous exhibition of prehistoric elephants. On the museum's first floor is Elephant Hall, where a herd of ten mounted elephants, mammoths, and mastodons awes visitors. This display is so striking that many visitors refer to the museum itself as "Elephant Hall."

There are countless other fascinating paleontology exhibits in the building, and many of them recall the Age of Dinosaurs. Mounted skeletons include those of a *Stegosaurus* and *Allosaurus* as well as large marine reptiles such as plesiosaurs and mosasaurs. Also on display are skulls or partial skeletons of *Triceratops*, *Tyrannosaurus rex*, and many other dinosaurs along with an abundance of material from the Cenozoic period and the Ice Age. It should be noted that only a fraction of the museum's collection of vertebrate fossils is actually on exhibit. The entire collection includes more than a million numbered specimens, most of them from the late Cenozoic. Many of these materials were quarried in Nebraska and adjoining states.

Another outstanding exhibition here is the Hall of Nebraska Wildlife. It includes sixteen dioramas depicting natural scenes from across the state. These dioramas, like many of the other exhibits at Morrill Hall, are interactive or include items that can be touched—a feature especially attractive to children.

> Nebraska State Museum of Natural History
> 307 Morrill Hall
> University of Nebraska
> Lincoln, NE 68588
> (402) 472-2642
> www.museum.unl.edu

Wyo-Braska Museum

The museum's unusual name derives from its location—smack on the Nebraska-Wyoming border. It features an abundance of

*A*S MUCH *as thirty feet long and weighing more than thirty tons, the* Baluchiterium *is the largest land mammal known to science. It looked something like an elephant without the trunk, only much larger. These strange creatures roamed the Asian forests and plains about thirty-five million years ago. In sheer*

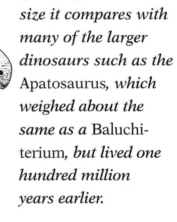

size it compares with many of the larger dinosaurs such as the Apatosaurus, *which weighed about the same as a* Baluchiterium, *but lived one hundred million years earlier.*

BALUCHITERIUM

mounted zoological specimens, many of them the same creatures pioneers would have seen as they traversed the nearby Oregon Trail in wagons. There are also a number of mammoth bones and other fossils from the Late Cenozoic and Ice Age. Of special interest is a full-size replica of a *Baluchiterium*, an extinct mammal that stood up to nineteen feet tall and reached a length of thirty feet. The *Baluchiterium* was as large as many, if not most, dinosaurs. The Wyo-Braska compares and contrasts this strange creature to the *Triceratops*, which inhabited these plains tens of millions of years before the *Baluchiterium* lumbered across it.

Wyo-Braska Museum
P.O. Box 623
950 U Street
Gering, NE 69341
(308) 436-7104

NORTH DAKOTA

University of North Dakota/Dakota Dinosaur Museum

A *Triceratops* serves as logo for the Dakota Dinosaur Museum, and just outside the museum entrance, you can meet one. A full-size *Triceratops* model created by a well-known western artist guards the door. Inside the 13,400-square-foot museum a *Velociraptor*, *Archaeopteryx*, saber-toothed cat, and several other life-size models or mounted skeletons await inspection by visitors. These dinos and other fossil exhibits offer a sampling of the more than three thousand specimens housed here. Many of the fossils were drawn from a dig not far from Dickinson and others from the dinosaur-rich Hell Creek rock formation found in parts of North and South Dakota and neighboring Montana.

University of North Dakota/Dakota Dinosaur
Museum
200 Museum Drive
Dickinson, ND 58601
(701) 225-DINO
www.dakotadino.com

University of North Dakota/Leonard Hall Museum

The University of North Dakota Geology Department maintains a small museum in the lobby of Leonard Hall. Dino-hunters will find here a variety of dinosaur remains including a *Triceratops*

167

skull, but the museum's most interesting fossil display may be the building itself. The limestone in the walls is shot through with fossil material. Dinosaur silhouettes decorate the exterior.

University of North Dakota/Leonard Hall Museum
P.O. Box 8358
University Station
Grand Forks, ND 58202
(701) 777-2011
www.und.edu

OHIO

Caesar Creek Lake

Collectors of shark teeth, trilobites, and other marine fossils should visit the spillway above the dam at Caesar Creek Lake near Waynesville, Ohio. Armed with a permit from the local office of the U.S. Army Corps of Engineers, they can gather up a few of these fossils and keep them.

Caesar Creek Lake
U.S. Army Corps of Engineers/Caesar Creek Lake
4020 North Clarksville
Waynesville, OH 45068
(513) 897-1050

Cincinnati Museum of Natural History

For many years travelers gathered at the magnificent Art Deco Union Station in Cincinnati to board trains bound for destinations all across America. Nowadays, people throng to the beautiful old terminal to visit its educational complex. The handsomely refurbished terminal now houses the Cincinnati History Museum, Cincinnati Historical Society Library, Cinergy Children's Museum, and Omnimax theater. However, the terminal's most popular attraction is likely the Museum of Natural History and Science—after all, that's where they keep the dinosaur stuff.

Although the city's nature museum can trace its roots all the way back to 1818 when a group of local naturalists combined their collections for public display, it is a very up-to-date institution. State-of-the-art exhibits and hands-on activities make it a must-see for anyone who loves science. Of particular note here is a world-class exhibition called "Cincinnati's Ice Age: Clues Frozen in Time." Visitors walk through an ice cave and across tundra to get an idea of what conditions were like twenty thousand years ago when ice sheets extended all the way down to the Ohio River Valley. The bison, ground sloths, and saber-toothed cats on display here were well suited to that sort of environment.

Of special interest to dino-hunters is the museum's field expedition program. Amateurs are welcome as long as they pay a share of the costs. Participants help advance the cause of science while learning firsthand about paleontology.

Cincinnati Museum of Natural History
1301 Western Avenue
Cincinnati, OH 45203
(513) 287-7000
www.cincymuseum.org

Cleveland Museum of Natural History

A wonderful and all too often overlooked city, Cleveland can boast beautiful parks, an exciting waterfront, a world-class orchestra, and one of the nation's finest natural history museums. Dino-hunters in or around the state of Ohio should definitely put both the city and the museum on their itineraries.

The paleontology exhibits here are especially rewarding. Among the mounted specimens are examples of a predatory *Allosaurus*, duckbill *Anatosaurus*, mosasaur, mammoth, mastodon, and saber-toothed cat. There are also skulls or other fossil materials from *Stegosaurus*, *Triceratops*, the *T-rex*-like *Nanotyrannus*, and many other dinosaur species. But the star of the show is the seventy-two-foot-long *Haplocanthosaurus*. This huge sauropod skeleton was unearthed in Canon City, Colorado, by a team from the Cleveland Museum. In all, the museum's vertebrate paleontology collection includes more than seven thousand specimens. Many of them were found in Ohio's 360-million-year-old shale deposits and thus predate the time of the dinosaurs.

Cleveland Museum of Natural History
1 Wade Oval Drive
University Circle
Cleveland, OH 44106
(216) 231-4600
www.cmnh.org

S OMEWHAT SIMILAR to the Brachiosaurus, *the* Haplocanthosaurus *was a hefty sauropod with long forelimbs. Fossil remains of this plant-eater have been found near Canon City in Colorado. Like many other such long-necked, elephantine dinosaurs, it lived during the Late Jurassic.*

HAPLOCANTOSAURUS

Dayton Museum of Natural History/Discovery Museum

The Dayton Museum of Natural History and Dayton Children's Museum have merged to create a single entity called the Discovery Museum. Soon to be bolstered by a ten thousand-square-foot interactive learning center, the newly merged museum will include a planetarium and an indoor zoo. Many of the paleo materials at the Dayton Museum are fossils of sea life or Cenozoic mammals, but plans call for an expansion of the museum's dinosaur holdings.

> Dayton Museum of Natural
>   History/Discovery Museum
> 2600 DeWeese Parkway
> Dayton, OH 45414
> (513) 275-7431
> **www.ohio.gov/afc/daytonm.html**

McKinley Museum and National Memorial

The McKinley advertises itself this way: "It's a hands-on museum, just don't feed the dinosaurs." That's a motto sure to attract kids and dino-hunters, and they won't be disappointed by what the museum has to offer. "Alice," the museum's robotic *Allosaurus,* is worth the visit, but there is much more here to see and enjoy including a replica of an actual excavation complete with exposed fossils.

> McKinley Museum and National Memorial
> 800 McKinley Monument Drive NW
> Canton, OH 44708
> (330) 455-7043
> **www.mckinleymuseum.org**

Orton Geological Museum

Walking into this museum on the campus of Ohio State University in Columbus, one is confronted by the mounted skeleton of *Megalonyx jeffersoni*, a giant ground sloth seven feet tall, eleven feet long, and with menacing five-inch claws. The sloth is not, of course, a dinosaur, but it is impressive enough to be one.

Inside the museum are real dinosaur materials such as a full-size skull cast of a *Tyrannosaurus rex*. There are also *Archaeopteryx* fossils and a skull of a large armored Paleozoic fish that lived about four hundred million years ago. Fossils here are mainly from Precambrian, Ordovician, Silurian, and Carboniferous rock layers that predate the dinosaurs. Even so, there are plenty of fossils to see since the Orton Geology Museum serves as a major archive for specimens from throughout Ohio and the Midwest. Approximately three-quarters of the museum's million or more geology specimens are fossils. Even the building is worth studying—it was built with fossil-filled stone. Instead of gargoyles, the builders decorated the roof with the heads of prehistoric creatures.

Orton Geological Museum
Ohio State University
155 South Oval
Columbus, OH 43210
(614) 292-6896
www.geology.ohio-state.edu/facilities/museum

SOUTH DAKOTA

Badlands National Park

The Oglala Sioux conducted Ghost Dances here during the 1890s and certainly there is something magical about the terrain. As if blasted by some titanic primordial explosion, the

172

grassy prairie breaks into a vast maze of buttes, pinnacles, and spires producing a scene so stark and barren that one wonders if anything could ever have lived here. The truth is, many creatures make their homes in the badlands today just as many others have done in the past. In fact, it was once a lush subtropical forest and before that a shallow sea teeming with life.

Today the land has sharply eroded, exposing the remains of the plants and animals that lived and died here during the Late Cretaceous and Cenozoic. The 244,000-acre Badlands National Park encompasses one of the largest and richest fossil beds on earth. Much of the fossil material found in these beds dates to the Oligocene epoch some twenty to thirty-five million years ago. Paleontologists continue to use these badlands fossils to study the evolution of the rhinoceros, horse, sheep, and countless other mammals.

Park visitors will want to drive the park's loop road, for not only will they see the fossil beds and spectacular scenery, but also bison, pronghorn, coyote, and bighorn sheep. Nature trails provide close-up views and interpretation. More than a million visitors pass through the park each year, so it should come as no surprise that disturbing or removing fossils or plants is prohibited.

Badlands National Park
P.O. Box 6
Interior, SD 57750
(605) 433-5361
www.badlands.national-park.com

Black Hills Institute of Geological Research

A private, for-profit paleontological organization, the Black Hills Institute of Geological Research sells professionally prepared fossils and museum-quality cast replicas. The

Institute is a thriving concern with sixteen geologists and preparers on staff. Storage, preparation, and display facilities are located in a five-building complex in Hill City, South Dakota. Exhibitors often turn to the Institute's extensive catalog when preparing displays.

Remarkably, Institute experts have excavated five different *Tyrannosaurus rex* skeletons. Among these was the controversial *T-rex* "Sue" that became the object of extensive litigation. Found on a Lakota Sioux ranch, the fossil bones were fought over by federal and tribal authorities, the ranch owner, and the Institute. The troublesome *T-rex* is now in the Field Museum in Chicago. Another Institute *T-rex*, nicknamed "Stan," is said to be the largest *Tyrannosaurus* skeleton ever mounted.

> Black Hills Institute of Geological Research
> P.O. Box 643
> 217 Main Street
> Hill City, SD 57745
> (605) 574-4289
> www.bhigr.com

Hot Springs Mammoth Site

The literature on this mammoth burial ground says it is "Where the big boys are." One would have to assume there are a few "big girls" as well since more than fifty woolly and Colombian mammoths have been excavated here—enough to be sure that some, at least, were female. Apparently the unfortunate mammoths frequently slipped and fell into the sinkhole created by the hot springs. Probably the visitors center and the excavation sites here can boast the largest concentration of mammoth fossils in the world.

*P*ERHAPS THE *best known of the Pleistocene mega-mammals is the elephant-like mammoth, which grew up to fifteen feet tall and weighed several tons. Some had thick hair, perhaps to help them survive the cold and harsh winds during the Ice Age. Mammoths lived in the northern latitudes of Europe, Asia, and North America, ranging across open plains, savannas, and through broken forests, much as modern elephants do in Africa today. They might have survived the end of the Ice Age if not for their likely vulnerability to human hunters. Some children mistakenly believe mammoths were dinosaurs.*

MAMMOTH

175

Hot Springs Mammoth Site
P.O. Box 692
Hot Springs, SD 57747
(605) 745-6017
www.mammothsite.com

South Dakota School of Mines Geology Museum

A teaching and research facility, this geology museum is used primarily by scientists and students at the South Dakota School of Mines. However, members of the general public are welcome, and there are some outstanding specimens on display. Remarkably, the complete museum collection includes more than 250,000 vertebrate fossils. Most were drawn from the nearby Black Hills and the White River Badlands region. The museum recently expanded its interpretive roll with the opening of The Journey, a new exhibit hall in Rapid City. Among its highlights are mounted skeletons of *Allosaurus* and *Camptosaurus*. Internet dino-hunters can access some excellent photographs of museum specimens at the address listed below.

South Dakota School of Mines Geology Museum
501 East Saint Joseph Street
Rapid City, SD 57701
(605) 394-2467
www.sdsmt.edu

Wall Drug Dino/Dinosaur Park

Dino-hunters and paleontology buffs on the loose in South Dakota will find plenty of opportunities to pursue their interests at the Badlands National Park, Hot Springs Mammoth Site, and elsewhere. When taking a break from their more serious scientific pursuits, they can also find places to have plenty of plain ol' fun with dinos. For instance, there is an eighty-foot-long Brontosaurus (or Apatosaurus, if you insist) just outside the Wall Drugstore in the town of Wall, South Dakota, off Interstate 90 to the east of Rapid City. The big sauropod is painted green and white and is a favorite of tourists. With its old-fashioned general store atmosphere—and its big dino—Wall Drug attracts customers from all over. Anyway, nobody is likely to miss the place.

The prehistory is cast in concrete at Dinosaur Park on Skyline Drive in Rapid City. There you can picnic beside five huge dino replicas or climb around on them if you happen to be about eight years old and are of a mind to.

> Wall Drug Dino/Dinosaur Park
> Dinosaur Park
> Rapid City Chamber of Commerce
> P.O. Box 747
> Rapid City, SD 57709
> (605) 343-1744

or

> Wall Drug
> 510 Main Street
> Wall, SD 57790
> (605) 279-2175

WISCONSIN

University of Wisconsin Geology Museum

About two-thirds of the space at this university geology museum is devoted to fossils of one sort or another. They range from tiny brachiopods to a thirty-three-foot mounted skeleton of a duck-billed *Edmontosaurus*. There is also a large, *Triceratops*-like *Avacerotops*. Other key fossil displays include a mastodon skeleton, three-toed horse skeleton, toothed-whale skull, pre-historic rhinoceros skull, saber-toothed cat, mosasaur, and icthyosaur. The mineral collection is enormous and includes materials from around the globe.

University of Wisconsin Geology Museum
1215 West Dayton Street
Madison, WI 53706
(608) 262-2399
www.geology.wisc.edu/~museum

Dinos in
Oklahoma and Texas

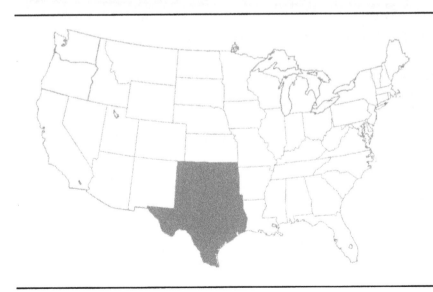

Cimarron Heritage Center

During the 1930s, paleontologist J. W. Stovall excavated some key Jurassic fossils in the Black Mesa of Oklahoma. He was assisted by road construction laborers, who had recently cut through a stretch of the fossil-rich Morrison Formation near the Cimarron River and discovered some huge bones. Most of the fossils discovered at Black Mesa were shipped to the Oklahoma Museum of Natural History in Norman, where some are now on display. A few others can be seen at the Cimarron Heritage Center in Boise City, Oklahoma. A concrete replica of a six-foot, 425-pound *Apatosaurus* femur marks the original roadside fossil quarry near Kenton. Incidentally, the Heritage Center is a fascinating place and well worth a visit. It celebrates the heroism of the hardy pioneers who settled the Cimarron Valley.

> Cimarron Heritage Center
> P.O. Box 655
> Boise City, OK 73933
> (580) 544-3479
> www.ptsi.net/users/museum

Oklahoma Museum of Natural History

This museum, located on the campus of the University of Oklahoma, is even older than the state of Oklahoma. It was created by the territorial legislature in 1899, eight years before Oklahoma became the forty-sixth state. During the century since, the museum's curators and staff have acquired more than five million artifacts and specimens. Among these are a large quantity of dinosaur materials, many of which will be highlighted in the museum's new Sam Noble Exhibition Building when its doors are opened soon.

The new building will offer fifty thousand square feet of public exhibit space with a substantial exhibition devoted to "Ancient Life." Therein visitors will see the world's largest *Apatosaurus* and *Pentaceratops* skeletons and a number of other mounted dinosaurs. The exhibition will emphasize Oklahoma's ever-changing environment and its impact on the life-and-death struggles of vertebrates such as the dinosaurs. Another key exhibition will tell the story of the "Peoples of Oklahoma."

A special museum feature will be its Pleistocene Plaza centered around a monumental sculpture of prehistoric Indians encountering a giant mammoth. This unusual space will overlook the naturally landscaped grounds of the museum. What better place to pause for a moment to contemplate the relationship of humans to their environment?

Interestingly, more than a few of the key fossils you'll see here were dug up by WPA workers during the Great Depression. While building a road near Kenton in the Black Mesa area of northwestern Oklahoma, the workers made an astonishing discovery. They unearthed a number of huge bones that seemed to be made out of solid rock. In fact, these were the fossilized remains of an *Apatosaurus*, then known as *Brontosaurus*. Noted paleontologist and Oklahoma Museum curator J. W. Stovall hurried to the site to conduct a scientific excavation. Many excellent specimens were removed only to be stored away in crates and eventually forgotten. During the 1980s, these fossils were rediscovered and "re-excavated" from their museum hiding place. They have now been placed on exhibit.

> Oklahoma Museum of Natural History
> 2401 Chatauqua
> Norman, OK 73072
> (405) 325-4712
> **www.omnh.ou.edu**

TEXAS

Archer Museum

This charming rural Texas Museum is located in the old Archer County Jailhouse in Archer City about twenty miles from Witchita Falls. Remember the little cowboy town depicted in Larry McMurtry's novels *The Last Picture Show* and *Texasville?* They were both made into hit movies. Well this is the very place they describe, more or less. Just look around a bit and you'll get the idea.

The museum contains about five thousand specimens and historical artifacts. The signs and labels on the displays were hand-painted, but the exhibits are no less fascinating than what you might see at, say, the Dallas Museum of Natural History—there are just fewer of them. For instance, you'll see a 280-million-year-old fern and a 100-million-year-old fossilized tree trunk, not to mention some antique farm equipment and drilling gear. The museum is open on weekends, but you'll need an appointment for weekday visits. The Archer's Web page is worth a look—you'll be amazed by the way this little downhome museum looks on the Internet.

*A*N EARLY *pterosaur, the* Rhamphorhynchus *had sharp teeth, a long tail, and powerful flight muscles attached to a spade-shaped breastplate. A kitelike membrane attached to the tail gave the animal added stability in flight. Flying reptiles of this type had disappeared by the end of the Jurassic.*

RHAMPHORHYNCHUS

Archer Museum
Archer City Chamber of Commerce
P.O. Box 877
Archer City, TX 76351
(940) 574-2489
www.archercity.org/museum

Big Bend National Park

Established in 1944, the Big Bend Park encompasses more than 800,000 acres of West Texas scrub and desert. It nearly fills the vast angle formed by the fabled Rio Grande as the river wanders southeastward and then bends sharply toward the north. This is a land of great beauty, a place where sunlight, rock, and vegetation combine to produce colors seen nowhere else on earth and where prickly pear cactus and wildflowers bloom on

*N*AMED FOR *a god worshiped by early Mexicans, this Griffin-like monster may have been the largest airborne creature in all of natural history. With a wingspan of forty feet or more, it was as big as a two-seater airplane, big enough in fact, to create a "blip" on a military radar screen. While most flying reptiles are thought to have lived near the coast, this one seems to have lived far inland. A university student is credited with having discovered the remains of* Quetzalcoatlus *in the Big Bend region of Texas.*

QUETZALCOATLUS

a schedule entirely their own. To a naturalist or to anyone with a touch of poetry in their hearts, Big Bend is pure magic. But to those hardy pioneers who tried to carve out an existence here, this harsh and unforgiving country was pure hell. Only a widely scattered handful of settlers survived here for long.

Some southwestern Indians hold that, when the Great Spirit had made the earth, all the leftover rocks were dumped onto the Big Bend. Park visitors are likely to agree that, sure enough, there are plenty of rocks here. This is a fact of considerable interest to dino-hunters since some of the stone layers exposed here contain important fossils. For instance, the first fossils of the huge flying lizard *Quetzalcoatlus* were found in the Big Bend by a University of Texas student.

If you come here on your own to search for prehistoric monsters, keep in mind that the law forbids disturbing or removing fossil material. You won't need it, since the memories you'll take with you when you leave the Big Bend will be more valuable than any rocks you are likely to find. This barren but exquisitely beautiful landscape conjures up remote prehistory—the appearance of the earth's dry land during the billions of years before life emerged from the seas. It is also easy to imagine that large parts of the prehistoric supercontinent Pangaea might have looked like this during the time of the dinosaurs.

> Big Bend National Park
> P.O. Box 129
> Big Bend National Park, TX 79834
> (915) 477-2251
> **www.big.bend.national-park.com**

Corpus Christi Museum of Science and History

Part of a complex of educational attractions called World of Discovery, the Corpus Christi Museum of Science and Technology features an entire hall devoted to earth science. The paleontology displays include dinosaur tracks, nests, and models. The grimacing *Tyrannosaurus rex* skull is a favorite with children—of course. And you'll also see a mounted mosasaur, a model of a flying reptile, and an assortment of Cenozoic mammals.

> Corpus Christi Museum of Science and History
> 1900 North Chaparral
> Corpus Christi, TX 78401
> (512) 883-2862

Dallas Museum of Natural History

Long a Dallas landmark, the Museum of Natural History in Fair Park is heavily oriented toward archaeology and—happily for us dino-hunters—paleontology. Founded in 1936, the museum can boast a collection of more than 280,000 fossils and other specimens. Among the many impressive displays is a *Tenontosaurus*, celebrated as the state's first mounted dinosaur skeleton. Also on exhibit here are *Mosasaurus* and *Glyptodon*, along with fossils of countless other fascinating prehistoric creatures. There are dinosaur tracks, as well as prehistoric fish, trilobites, and plenty of Cenozoic mammals. Elsewhere in the museum are dozens of wildlife dioramas depicting present-day habitats throughout Texas.

Many of the museum's offerings can be enjoyed, not just in its exhibit halls, but at its excellent Internet Web site as well. In fact, this Web site is among the most comprehensive and informative on the Internet. One especially attractive feature is its Paleobase, an on-line resource for both amateur and professional researchers. Paleobase provides photographs of key specimens in the museum collection and detailed information on species. The site also features an Interactive Identifier to help you find out about fossils you've collected in the field.

Dallas Museum of Natural History
3535 Grand Avenue
Dallas, TX 75210
(214) 421-3466
www.dallasdino.org

Dinosaur Valley State Park

The dinosaur tracks along the clean-flowing Paluxy River near Glen Rose, Texas, are justifiably among the most famous dinotracks in the world. The footprints were left in soft mud about 110 million years ago when this area stood near the shore of a primordial sea. They were made at about the same time by a sixty-foot-long sauropod, a thirty-foot-long duck-billed dinosaur,

186

*P*ART OF *a group of large carnivorous theropods called carnosaurs, the* Spinosaurus *was related to the* Allosaurus, Ceratosaurus, *and* Dilophosaurus. *Unlike most other carnosaurs, however, it had a six-foot-high, skin-covered sail on its back. In this way, it was similar to the* Dimetrodon, *which lived two hundred million years earlier and may have been an ancestor of the mammals. The sail may have helped the* Spinosaurus *regulate the temperature of its forty-foot-long body. When turned broadside to the sun, the sail would have absorbed heat quickly and warmed the animal. Then, during the heat of the day, the sail could be turned away from the sun, allowing it to dissipate unwanted heat.* Spinosaurus *fossils date to the Cretaceous, and have been found only in Africa.*

S
P
I
N
O
S
A
U
R
U
S

and a twelve-foot-long predatory theropod, which may have been in pursuit of the plant-eaters.

The park features a pair of fiberglass dinosaur models: an *Apatosaurus* and a *Tyrannosaurus rex*. There is also a small herd of longhorn cattle, which you may find nearly as much fun as the dinos. The park store offers rocks, fossils, and dinosaur souvenirs.

Dinosaur Valley State Park
P.O. Box 396
Glen Rose, TX 76043
(254) 897-4588
www.tpwd.state.tx.us/park/dinosaur/dinosaur.htm

Heard Natural Science Museum

Miss Bessie Heard (1884–1988) grew up around McKinney, Texas, and during her more than a century of life amassed a collection of natural specimens and odds and ends that could put many museums to shame. By the mid-1960s her shells, minerals, gems, and artifacts had filled her house to overflowing. So, in 1967, Miss Bessie and her friends in McKinney built a 25,000-square-foot museum to house the collection and make it more accessible to the public. Accompanying the museum is a 287-acre wildlife sanctuary, outdoor aquatic laboratory, and raptor rehabilitation center. The museum has over a dozen separate display areas, some of them devoted to prehistory. Among the best fossils on display here is a mosasaur skull.

Heard Natural Science Museum
One Nature Place
McKinney, TX 75069
(972) 562-5566
www.heardmuseum.org

Hondo Dinosaur Trackway

The town of Hondo takes its name from a Spanish word meaning "deep creek." Millions of years ago a herd of plant-eating dinosaurs passed this way and found the going very deep. The big feet of these fifteen-ton plant-eaters sank far into a layer of soft mud, creating prints that were later turned to stone by drying and compression. Discovered many years ago by settlers, these dino-footprints can be seen in the bed of Hondo Creek just off F.M. 462 about twenty miles north of town.

> Hondo Dinosaur Trackway
> Hondo Area Chamber of Commerce
> 1802 Avenue M
> Hondo, TX 78861
> (850) 426-3037
> **www.texas-on-line.com/graphic/hondo.htm**

Panhandle Plains Historical Museum

Located on the campus of West Texas A&M University in Canyon, the Panhandle Plains Historical Museum dates to 1933 when its Art Deco Pioneer Hall building was completed. As the museum's paleontology exhibits make quite clear, however, the surrounding plains themselves are considerably older. On display here are the fossils of the shovel-tusked mastodon, giant ground sloth, and saber-toothed cat as well as *Triceratops*. There is also a geology exhibit unveiling the story of the Amarillo Mountain Range, all of which is now weathered away and buried. Much of the museum is devoted to history exhibits, which tell the story of settlement and survival in the Texas Panhandle with exhibits on plains Indians, ranching, windmills, and oil development.

Panhandle Plains Historical Museum
West Texas A&M University
2401 Fourth Avenue
Canyon, TX 79016
(806) 651-2244
www.wtamu.edu/museum/home.html

Science Place

The staff at the Science Place in Dallas say they welcome "kids ages 1 to 109," and that's a lucky thing. The moving, roaring *T-rex* and other robot dinosaurs at this museum are a favorite with children whatever their ages. The museum also features an Imax theater and planetarium.

Science Place
P.O. Box 151469
Dallas, TX 75315
(214) 428-7200
www.scienceplace.org

Shuler Museum of Paleontology

This campus geology museum contains fossil specimens from around Texas and the world. Some were discovered by Dr. Louis Jacobs, one of SMU's star paleontologists.

Shuler Museum of Paleontology
Southern Methodist University
Department of Geological Science
P.O. Box 750395
3225 Daniel Avenue
Dallas, TX 75275
(214) 768-2750
www.smu.edu

Strecker Museum

A geology and natural history museum associated with Baylor University, the Strecker is part of a four-museum complex including a children's discovery center, a historic Texas village, and the site of a mammoth discovery near Waco. The beginnings of the Strecker date all the way back to 1856 when Baylor was located in tiny Independence, Texas. At that time the Strecker collections filled just a few cabinets and consisted of what were described as "rocks, mineral, and petrifactions." Today, the museum houses more than a few petrifactions—what we now call fossils. Among them are mammoth bones removed from excavations along the Brazos River in Waco. A new 100,000-square-foot display building has been proposed for the Baylor campus.

> Strecker Museum
> Fourth Street and Speight Avenue
> P.O. Box 97154
> Waco, TX 76798
> (254) 710-1110
> www.baylor.edu/Strecker_Museum/strecker.html

Texas Memorial Museum

The collections at the Texas Memorial Museum are almost as big as the state that spawned them. Located on the sprawling Austin campus of the University of Texas—one of the nation's largest educational institutions—the museum is crammed with millions upon millions of specimens. The non-vertebrate fossil collection alone exceeds 3.6 million specimens. Compare that to some of the other museums in this book, which may offer a few thousand or even a few hundred specimens.

191

The museum's non-vertebrate collection is likely the largest in the world, but its dinosaur holdings are more limited. Perhaps that is because much of Texas was underwater during the Age of Dinosaurs. Even so, one can see some unique dino-wonders here. Some of the best of them are located in a small building some distance from the main exhibit hall. Here are some of the famed dinosaur tracks collected from the bed of Paluxy Creek about five miles northwest of Glen Rose, Texas. One of the tracks is thought to have been made by a lumbering sauropod about sixty feet long and weighing as much as thirty tons. A second set of three-toed tracks were made by a twelve-foot theropod walking on its hind legs. Some scientists think the theropod was likely a meat-eater in pursuit of the larger sauropod.

The museum displays several excellent mounted mosasaur skeletons, one of them more than thirty feet long and with a skull almost five feet long. Its jaw was so formidable that it could take a three-foot bite out of anything it attacked. Other impressive fossils in the museum include those of the giant flying reptile *Quetzalcoatlus*, the *Apatosaurus*-like *Diplodocus*, and the sail-backed *Dimetrodon*, which predated the dinosaurs and may have been an ancestor to early mammals.

Texas Memorial Museum
University of Texas
2400 Trinity Street
Austin, TX 78705
(512) 471-1604
www.utexas.edu/depts/tmm

Texas Tech University Museum

Founded in 1929, this museum was first housed in the basement of a building on campus. Today it fills a substantial facility on

Fourth and Indian Streets in Lubbock and has spread its wings sufficiently to include a major planetarium, a natural science research center, and a key archaeological landmark. The museum holds almost two million specimens and artifacts in its collections. The one most likely to interest dino-hunters is the mounted skeleton of a twenty-five-foot *Allosaurus*. There are many other fascinating fossils and casts as well.

Dr. William Curry Holden, the museum's first curator, was known for having identified the first Folsom projectile points discovered in the Lubbock Lake area. The site of that discovery is now a historic landmark and an internationally recognized center for the study of early man in the Americas.

> Texas Tech University Museum
> Fourth and Indiana
> Lubbock, TX 79409
> (806) 742-2490
> **www.ttu.edu/~museum**

Witte Museum of History and Science

The big dinosaur attraction at this Alamo City museum is the mounted *Triceratops* skeleton on display just inside the entrance.

> Witte Museum of History and Science
> 3801 Broadway
> San Antonio, TX 78209
> (210) 357-1900
> **www.wittemuseum.org**

Dinos in
the Four Corners

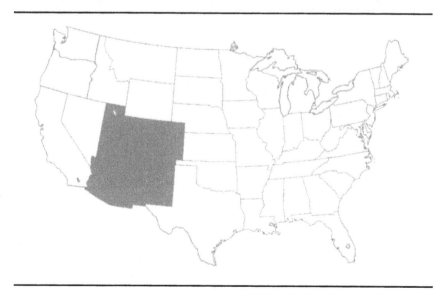

Arizona Science Center

Located right in the middle of downtown Phoenix, this museum probes many fields of science including paleontology. Dinosaurs are not a major theme here, but dino-hunters will find two very impressive skull casts of *Tyrannosaurus rex* and *Triceratops*. Skulls are about all that is required to tell the story of these two giant Cretaceous antagonists. You don't have to see the whole skeleton to get a feeling for their size or the violence of their likely confrontations.

> Arizona Science Center
> 7th and Washington Streets
> Phoenix, AZ 85004
> (602) 716-2000
> www.azscience.org

Mesa Southwest Museum

In addition to its extensive archaeological holdings, the museum houses a number of paleontology exhibits including the popular "Jurassic Arizona." Dino-hunters may want to ask about the Southwest Paleontology Society, a volunteer organization associated with the museum. The society consists of amateurs and

VS

*I*N THE *popular imagination, these two giants are forever locked in mortal combat. Paleontologists agree that they were likely predator-versus-prey competitors in the struggle for survival. Scientists believe the* Triceratops *may have run across the Late Cretaceous landscape in sizable herds, much as the American bison did before being decimated by hunters during the tenth century. Probably, pack-hunting meat-eaters such as the* T-rex *harassed the herds, picking off young, weak, or unwary animals whenever opportunity presented itself. However, the formidable horns and head armor of an adult* Triceratops *would have made direct confrontations extremely difficult and dangerous, even for the dauntless* Tyrannosaurus rex.

T-rex

TRICERATOPS

197

professionals interested in the field of paleontology, and of course, dinosaurs are an important focus.

> Mesa Southwest Museum
> 53 North Macdonald Street
> Mesa, AZ 85201
> (602) 644-2230
> www.ci.mesa.az.us

Museum of Northern Arizona

Founded in 1928 by local citizens, the Museum of Northern Arizona collects and displays cultural artifacts and natural history specimens from the Colorado Plateau. Also known as the Four Corners, the plateau encompasses 130,000 square miles of mesas, canyons, and rocky, monument-like buttes, often reddish in color. Traveling in this breathtaking country gives one a strong sense of the passage of time and the power of geological change.

This area has yielded countless valuable fossils to dinosaur hunters, and not a few of them have ended up at the museum. Among the highlights of the museum is a life-size skeletal model of a *Dilophosaurus*, a particularly vicious carnivore.

The museum's anthropology exhibit is also well worth a close look since it, too, celebrates the timelessness of the region. More than twelve thousand years of human occupation are documented. While that may seem like a long time to us, consider that the dinosaurs disappeared sixty-five million years before humans first hunted and raised crops here.

> Museum of Northern Arizona
> Fort Valley Road
> P.O. Box 720
> Flagstaff, AZ 86001
> (520) 774-5213
> www.mna.com

*A*MONG THE *first large meat-eating dinosaurs, the twenty-foot-long* Dilophosaurus *lived during the early Jurassic about 190 million years ago. Like many of the other carnivorous theropods that came afterward, it ran on two legs and had extremely sharp teeth. The male* Dilophosaurus *had a pair of thin, bony ridges on its head. Possibly, this strange-looking crest was used to attract females or warn off competing males.*

DILOPHOSAURUS

Tuba City Dinosaur Tracks

Just off Highway 160 to the north of the Painted Desert is one of the nation's more dramatic dinosaur trackways. The prints were left in soft mud by a herd of bipedal carnivores who came this way during the Early Jurassic, about two hundred million years ago. These are believed to have been *Dilophosaurus*, three-toed creatures that walked or ran on two legs and stood about ten feet tall. While they were not huge by dinosaur standards, it is nonetheless a lucky thing for modern visitors that these ferocious meat-eaters went on their way long ago, leaving behind nothing but their footprints.

> Tuba City Dinosaur Tracks
> U.S. 160 about five miles west
> of Tuba City, Arizona

University of Arizona Mineralogical Museum

An extensive collection of rocks, minerals, meteorites, and gemstones make this university museum a mecca for rock hounds and geologists. It holds less attraction for dino-hunters, who may nonetheless benefit from learning as much about geology as possible. The museum maintains and displays a respectable selection of fossils.

> University of Arizona Mineralogical Museum
> Flandrau Science Center
> 1601 East University
> Tuscon, AZ 85721
> (520) 621-4227
> **www.flandrau.org**
> **www.arizona.edu/services/museums/museums.html**

COLORADO

Dry Mesa Quarry

One of the world's most famous fossil deposits, the Dry Mesa Quarry is the site of several groundbreaking dinosaur discoveries. Not the least of these were *Supersaurus* and *Ultrasaurus*, among the largest land animals known to science. Complete skeletons have never been found, but fragmentary fossil evidence indicates that these plant-eating sauropods ranged up to 140 feet in length—nearly half as long as a football field. The Museum of Western Colorado and other paleontological facilities in the region may have information on visits or guided tours of the quarry. Visitors are cautioned to leave this sensitive scientific reserve undisturbed.

Dry Mesa Quarry, U.S. Forest Service
2250 Highway 50
Delta, CO 81416
(970) 249-1726

Florissant Fossil Beds National Monument

About thirty-five million years ago, long after the dinosaurs had disappeared, a sapphire-blue lake stretched for fifteen miles through what is now known as the Florissant Valley. Lush growth and towering redwoods covered the hillsides around the lake. Then a nearby volcano exploded, dumping millions of tons of ash and mud onto the lake, burying fish and wildlife and smothering the surrounding trees and greenery. Over time, sediments produced by this and similar eruptions built up a thick layer of fossil-bearing shale.

Today, the shale deposits at Florissant are an invaluable resource for scientists studying plant life and insects of the Oligocene epoch (25–40 million years ago). The fossilized remains of a thousand-plus insects and more than a hundred plant species have been recovered here.

Although you'll see no dinosaur fossils, a visit to Florissant Fossil Beds National Monument west of Colorado Springs is well worthwhile. The scenic fossil beds and exhibits at the visitors center provide insight into the study of ancient life. Especially fascinating is a mile-long hike through a forest of petrified redwood trunks.

Florissant Fossil Beds National Monument
P.O. Box 185
Florissant, CO 80816
(719) 748-3253
www.nps.gov/flfo

Garden Park Paleontology Society/Dinosaur Depot

Headquartered in Canon City, Colorado, the Garden Park Paleontology Society draws strength and prestige from a long
dinosaur-hunting tradition. In 1876, a local schoolteacher
made a discovery that would help spark the "bone wars" of the
late nineteenth century. While walking in a local park, he came
across a cache of very large fossil material, which turned out to
be dinosaur bones. The find brought rival teams of collectors
hurrying to Canon City where they unearthed truckloads of
fossils. Their work led to the identification of seventeen new
dinosaur species including the heavily plated *Stegosaurus*. Even
today, important fossil discoveries continue to be made here.

In 1995 the Society opened an education and display center
called Dinosaur Depot, where visitors can learn more about the
original Garden Park finds and the prehistory of southern Colorado. Offerings include a working paleontology lab, regularly
scheduled family programs, tours of the Garden Park dinosaur
quarry, and of course, plenty of fossils. The center also offers
training for paleontology field and lab work.

> Garden Park Paleontology Society/Dinosaur Depot
> 330 Royal Gorge Boulevard
> P.O. Box 1957
> Canon City, CO 81215
> (719) 269-7150
> www.coloradodirectory.com/dinosaurdepot

Morrison Natural History Museum/Dinosaur Ridge

A layer of unusually rich fossil-bearing rock runs beneath several western states. Called the Morrison Formation, it dates to
the Late Jurassic period, at which time it was a vast floodplain
covered in lush vegetation and alive with dinosaurs. Now more

than 140 million years old, the formation takes its name from the little town of Morrison located in the foothills of the Rockies just west of Denver. A massive outcropping of the reddish Morrison Formation can be seen just outside of town, and it was here in 1877 that schoolteacher Arthur Lakes found the fossils that touched off the great American bone wars.

In Morrison itself a small but well-run natural history museum celebrates the importance of the town and its namesake rock layer to the science of paleontology. Museum displays recount the story of how Lakes, while out for a bracing hike in the foothills of the Rockies, made his historic discovery. Lakes notified both the wealthy collector O. C. Marsh and rival fossil hunter E. D. Cope of his find. Naturally, both of these bone warriors were desperate to get their hands on the Lakes material, but Marsh had first claim, and he eventually paid the teacher $100 for the fossils. Tours of the historic Dinosaur Ridge dig sites are conducted by volunteer museum staff.

Morrison Natural History Museum/Dinosaur Ridge
P.O. Box 564
Morrison, CO 80465
(303) 697-1873
(303) 697-DINO
town.morrison.co.us/mnhm.html

Purgatory Dinosaur Tracks

These extraordinary dinosaur trackways lie far in the Colorado backcountry and can only be reached by means of a guided jeep tour or a rugged fifteen-mile hike. Although remote, the trackways are well worth the effort. More than 1,200 tracks laid down by a number of different species have been found here. Seeing them, it is easy to imagine the huge creatures lumbering along through the soft mud—now turned to stone.

Purgatory Dinosaur Tracks
Comanche National Grasslands
1420 East Third Street
La Junta, CO 81050
(719) 384-2181

Rabbit Valley Trail Through Time/ Museum of Western Colorado

Just off I-70 about two miles east of the Utah border, the Museum of Western Colorado and Bureau of Land Management maintain an active dinosaur quarry. Visitors are welcome to view and enjoy the area by hiking the moderately strenuous 1.5-mile "Trail Through Time." The walk will take you through a rich fossil-bearing stratum dating to Jurassic times, and dinosaur fossils can be seen in the rocks at the side of the trail. However, you are cautioned to leave them as they are for scientists to study and other dino-hunters to enjoy.

Along the way you'll see plenty of modern vegetation such as rabbit brush, prickly pear, hedge cactus, and juniper, and wildlife such as coyote, ground squirrels, a variety of snakes and lizards, and of course, rabbits. Take your time and use your imagination to contrast the scene as it looks now with how it must have looked 140 million years ago during the Jurassic. Long ago, this was not desert country, but rather a swampy floodplain lush with tall conifers and ferns and alive with insects, crocodiles, turtles, and—you guessed it—dinosaurs!

Rabbit Valley Trail Through Time
Bureau of Land Management
2815 H Road
Grand Junction, CO 81506
(970) 244-3000

or

*A*MONG THE *better known and more easily recognized types of dinosaur is the* Stegosaurus *("Roofed Lizard"). The pointed plates running the length of its back and tail are quite distinctive, but probably were of little use for defense. Instead, they likely served as heat exchangers to help the animal regulate its body temperature. The slow-moving* Stegosaurus *had a set of sharp spikes on the end of its whiplike tail to keep predators at a distance. A Late Jurassic plant-eater some twenty to thirty feet in length, it left fossils in Colorado and a number of other western states.*

Since the Stegosaurus *was first discovered and described during the 1870s, scientists have been scratching their heads over the arrangement of the spines on its back. Were they staggered or arranged in matching pairs? Concerning the intelligence of this creature, however, there is little controversy. Its cranial cavity was only large enough for a brain of less than three ounces. One must assume that it never needed to do a lot of thinking.*

STEGOSAURUS

Museum of Western Colorado
248 South 4th Street
P.O. Box 20000
Grand Junction, CO 81502
(970) 242-0971
www.mwc.mus.co.us/dinosaurs/rabbit.htm

Riggs Hill Dinosaur Trail/Museum of Western Colorado

A short trail not far from Grand Junction provides access to Riggs Hill where several historically important dinosaur fossil discoveries were made. Early specimens of *Stegosaurus*, *Allosaurus*, and *Brachiosaurus* were uncovered here. Just under a mile in length, the trail leads hikers to the top of Riggs Hill, from which they can view the entire fossil-strewn Grand Valley of the Colorado and Gunnison Rivers. Unfortunately, souvenir hunters have removed so much fossil bone from the area that it has lost much of its importance as a scientific resource.

Riggs Hill Dinosaur Trail
Bureau of Land Management
2815 H Road
Grand Junction, CO 81506
(970) 244-3000

or

Museum of Western Colorado
248 South 4th Street
P.O. Box 20000
Grand Junction, CO 81502
(970) 242-0971
www.mwc.mus.co.us/dinosaurs/riggs.htm

University of Colorado Museum

As befitting an institution located in the heart of the fossil-rich Rocky Mountain region, the University of Colorado takes pride in its paleontology collections and exhibits. On display at the university's museum in Boulder are skulls of several large dinosaurs, including *Diplodocus* and *Triceratops*, along with many other major fossils. However, the museum's complete fossil collection extends far beyond what you see on display. Much of it is stored away and accessible only to researchers and students. The complete collection includes more than 95,000 cataloged specimens, most, though by no means all, of them drawn from the Rocky Mountain region. Some collections of Cretaceous invertebrates, mollusks, and insects are considered historically important. An especially fine fossil egg collection was drawn from sites throughout the world.

> University of Colorado Museum
> University of Colorado
> Campus Box 218
> Boulder, CO 80309
> (303) 492-6892
> www.colorado.edu/CUMUSEUM

New Mexico

Clayton Lake State Park

Set amid rolling grasslands in far northeastern New Mexico, Clayton Lake State Park offers excellent trout and bass fishing. It also features an extraordinary 100-million-year-old dinosaur trackway consisting of more than five hundred footprints. A short trail provides a view of the tracks, made during the Cretaceous by at least five different species of dinosaur. Some of the prints may have been made by juvenile dinosaurs.

> Clayton Lake State Park
> Route 370
> Clayton, NM 88415
> (505) 374-8808
> www.emnrd.state.nm.us/nmparks

Farmington Museum

Located smack in the middle of the Four Corners region, home of many dinosaur attractions, Farmington, New Mexico, and its municipal museum are well worth a stopover. While you won't find a lot of dinosaur material here, there are some interesting fossils, and the museum's geology exhibits help put the Four Corners prehistory in perspective. The Children's Gallery has plenty of interactive displays, games, and toys to keep kids of any age happy. The museum store sells fossils as well as gems, crystals, and assorted minerals.

> Farmington Museum
> 302 North Orchard
> Farmington, NM 87401
> (505) 599-1179
> www.fmtn.org

New Mexico Museum of Natural History

New Mexico is big dinosaur country. Dinosaurs lived here from about 225 million years ago, when they first appeared in the planetary fossil record, right down until the end of the Cretaceous some 65 million years ago, an astounding 160-million-year period. Dinosaur fossils were first collected in New Mexico during the 1880s and they continue to be found today. Since then, the remains of *Stegosaurus, Allosaurus, Camarasaurus, Albertosaurus, Coelophysis, Parasaurolophus,* and many other species have been unearthed here. Recent finds include those of newly discovered dinosaurs such as the small, plant-eating *Revueltosaurus* and the titanic *Seismosaurus.*

The New Mexico Museum of Natural History in Albuquerque takes full advantage of the state's rich dinosaur heritage. Its dinosaur exhibits are among the finest in the

Southwest. Mounted skeletons, models, or fossil remains of all the wondrous species mentioned above are on display. Museum personnel are especially proud of the *Seismosaurus* fossils exhibited in the Jurassic Hall. A monster plant-eater some forty meters long, the *Seismosaurus* was unknown to science until fossil specimens were unearthed near San Ysidro during the early 1980s. Perhaps the museum's most attractive feature is its "Fossilworks," a public display area where trained volunteers process fossils and prepare them for storage or exhibit. Even highly valuable *Seismosaurus* fossils have been prepared here.

The museum's Web site is excellent and contains considerable information on New Mexico dinosaurs. It can be accessed at the address below.

> New Mexico Museum of Natural History
> 1801 Mountain Road NW
> Albuquerque, NM 87104
> (505) 841-2802
> **www.nmmnh-abq.mus.nm.us**

New Mexico Tech Mineralogical Museum

The region around Socorro has a rugged, primordial appearance that suggests antiquity. The approximately ten thousand specimens in this small university mineral museum make a stop here well worth your while. So, too, does the majesty of the surrounding countryside. Each winter huge numbers of cranes, snow geese, and other birds gather along the Rio Grande near Socorro. If you happen to be looking for living dinosaurs, birds are as close as you'll come.

> New Mexico Tech Mineralogical Museum
> Socorro, NM 87801
> (505) 835-5420 or (800) 428-TECH
> **www.nmt.edu**

Ruth Hall Museum of Paleontology

The richly colored rocks and desert hills of New Mexico's Ghost Ranch conjure images of the supercontinent Pangaea as it might have looked when dinosaurs roamed the earth. Part of an old Spanish land grant dating back to 1766, the twenty-one thousand-acre ranch was given to the Presbyterian Church during the 1950s. Today it is the site of a noted educational facility and conference center.

The Ghost Ranch Center—its name comes from a number of ghostly legends associated with the ranch—offers three fascinating museums. The Florence Hawley Ellis Museum tells the story of the twelve thousand years of human habitation in this region through Native American, Spanish, and Anglo art. The Ghost Ranch Living Museum provides insight into local geology and wildlife—a mountain lion and other live animals native to the ranch can be seen here. But the place dino-hunters will most want to see is the Ruth Hall Museum of Paleontology. It features more than a hundred articulated fossil skeletons including those of a number of Triassic dinosaurs. Perhaps the most important of these are remains of *Coelophysis*, a small carnivore that inhabited this region about 225 million years ago. The Ghost Ranch was the site of a major paleontology find during the 1940s when a large number of *Coelophysis* skeletons were uncovered here. The quarry where these fossils were found is accessible.

Ruth Hall Museum of Paleontology
Ghost Ranch Conference Center
HC 77, Box 11
Abiquiu, NM 87510
(505) 685-4333
www.newmexico-ghostranch.org/museums.html

University of New Mexico Geology Museum

Located in the University of New Mexico's Northrop Hall, this small museum features minerals and fossils from the state, the Southwest, and around the world. While there are many interesting fossils on exhibit, dinosaurs are not the main focus here. The museum's mineral collection includes one of the largest meteorites ever recovered.

> University of New Mexico Geology Museum
> Albuquerque, NM 87131
> (505) 277-4204
> www.unm.edu

UTAH

Brigham Young University Earth Science Museum

The BYU Earth Science Museum is home to one of the best and most extensive Jurassic fossil collections in America. However, only a small fraction of the collection is actually on display at the museum. Among the exhibits are mounted skeletons of *Allosaurus* and *Camptosaurus*, a 150-million-year-old dinosaur egg, and an extensive mural depicting the Utah-Colorado region during the Jurassic period. A special attraction is a fossil table where you are allowed to pick up and examine the specimens.

> Brigham Young University Earth Science Museum
> P.O. Box 23300
> 1683 North Canyon Road
> Provo, UT 84602
> (801) 378-3680
> www.byu.edu

211

*D*URING RECENT *decades, fossil evidence of several new types of sauropod have been located in the western United States. As if driven by a sort of paleontological "Pentagon mentality," scientists have competed with one another to find the largest possible sauropod specimen. Among their discoveries are the* Supersaurus, Ultrasaurus, *and largest of all,* Seismosaurus *("Earthquake Lizard"). All are related to the Late Jurassic* Diplodocus, *which at twelve tons or more was itself a sizable animal. But the* Seismosaurus *was one whale of a lot bigger. The largest land animal yet known to science, the* Seismosaurus *grew as much as 130 feet long and weighed over 100 tons—more than 200,000 pounds! To say the least, a herd of these titanic beasts on the move would have shaken the ground. Their size alone was probably enough to protect them from all predators.*

S E I S M O S A U R U S

Cleveland-Lloyd Dinosaur Quarry

About thirty miles south of Price, Utah, is one of the most productive dinosaur quarries in the world. Since 1929, when scientists first began to dig here, the Cleveland-Lloyd Dinosaur Quarry has yielded more than twelve thousand fossil specimens. Over the years, paleontologists and collectors from Princeton, the University of Utah, and other institutions have

212

steadily worked the quarry, unearthing the remains of at least seventy animals representing fourteen different Jurassic species.

The quarry is especially rich in fossils related to the *Allosaurus*, a bipedal Jurassic predator. Because so many *Allosaurus* skeletons have been unearthed here, this animal is particularly well represented in museum exhibits. Fossils from the Cleveland-Lloyd Quarry are now on display in more than sixty museums around the globe.

The land surrounding the quarry is bone-dry nowadays, but about 150 million years ago this place was a large fresh-water lake. Apparently, its shallows concealed a thick layer of sticky mud that fatally trapped any creature straying too far from the shore. Both plant-eaters and the carnivores that preyed on them became trapped, leaving their bones to be discovered by modern humans.

The visitors center contains a mounted *Allosaurus* and a *Stegosaurus*. Since this important fossil bed remains of interest to scientists, you may see crews at work uncovering and removing fossils.

> Cleveland-Lloyd Dinosaur Quarry
> Bureau of Land Management
> 125 South 600 Street West
> Price, UT 84501
> (435) 636-3600
> **www.utah.com**

Dead Horse Point State Park

Few state parks anywhere in America provide so spectacular a view as this one in southeastern Utah. Dead Horse Point itself is a narrow neck of land created by the prehistoric meanderings of the Colorado River. Over many millions of years, the river has carved out a deep canyon on three sides of the point, leaving a rocky crest some two thousand feet above the water. The Point got its rather grim name from a group of wild mustangs that were stranded on the point and died of thirst here. The park visitors center, located off Highway 191 north of Moab, has a number of fossils and early Native American artifacts on display. But the big attraction here is Dead Horse Point itself. The land is so barren and so stark in its beauty that one cannot help but imagine this is what much of our planet looked like before the first life emerged from the seas.

Dead Horse Point State Park
P.O. Box 609
Moab, UT 84532
(801) 259-2614
www.utah.com

Dinosaur Museum

While in the Four Corners region, dino-hunters won't want to miss the Dinosaur Museum in Blanding. On hand are mounted skeletons, fossilized skin, eggs, footprints, and some of the most delightful graphic depictions of dinosaurs you'll see anywhere. Models, sculptures, or fossil materials from *Tyrannosaurus rex*, *Allosaurus*, *Stegosaurus*, *Deinonychus*, *Tarbosaurus* (an Asia cousin of the *T-rex*), and many other types and species can be seen here. The folks who run this museum haven't forgotten that dinosaurs are fun. For instance, there is an entire exhibition devoted to movie dinos from the 1925 classic *The Lost World* right up to *Jurassic Park* and its sequel, also called *Lost World*.

Dinosaur Museum
745 South 200 West
Blanding, UT 84511
(435) 678-3454
www.utah.com

*A*LTHOUGH MAMMALS *appeared at about the same time as dinosaurs, they remained in the shadow of their larger and more numerous reptilian competitors for more than 150 million years—in fact, right down until the dinosaurs disappeared at the end of the Cretaceous period some sixty-five million years ago. Among the reasons for this may be the presence of small predatory dinosaurs such as the* Coelophysis. *Only about ten feet long from head to tail, this Late Triassic meat-eater weighed about fifty pounds and was quite agile. It likely hunted in large packs and made a steady diet of hapless mammals.* Coelophysis *fossils have been found in New Mexico, New England, and Africa.*

COELOPHYSIS

Eastern Utah Prehistoric Museum

A substantial quantity of the material removed from the incredibly rich Cleveland-Lloyd Dinosaur Quarry ended up in the Prehistoric Museum at the College of Eastern Utah in Price. As a result, the fossil collection at this small college museum is nothing short of fantastic. You'll see handsome skeleton mounts or fossils of *Camptosaurus, Camarasaurus, Chasmosaurus, Stegosaurus, Allosaurus, Prosaurolophus* (one of many hadrosaur-like plant-eating species), and the exceedingly rare *Utahraptor*, with its razor-sharp slashing claw. Also on hand is a model of Gastonia Burgei, a creature named for the museum's curator. There are also excellent exhibits on Cenozoic animals and the prehistoric peoples of North America.

Eastern Utah Prehistoric Museum
College of Eastern Utah
155 East Main
Price, UT 84501
(435) 637-5060
www.utah.com

Escalante State Park

Perhaps 140 million years ago a logjam piled up on a river near what is now the town of Escalante, Utah. The logs were covered over by sand and gravel and were slowly mineralized and hardened to stone as crystals filled the cells of the wood. Many of these prehistoric trees are now exposed and can be seen at the side of trails in Escalante State Park. Not far from the park visitors center is Petrified Wood Cove, a rock garden where many of the colorful logs are displayed. The center also has dinosaur fossils and prehistoric Indian artifacts on exhibit.

Escalante State Park
710 North Reservoir Road
Escalante, UT 84726
(435) 826-4466
www.nr.state.ut.us/parks/www1/esca.htm

George Eccles Dinosaur Park

The Ogden River Parkway starts at the mouth of a spectacular canyon and ends in downtown Ogden, Utah. Along the way, hikers and bikers will enjoy some lovely scenery, but their biggest thrill comes about halfway along the route when they enter the George Eccles Dinosaur Park. There they encounter life-size replicas of dinos and reptiles from throughout the Triassic, Jurassic, and Cretaceous Periods.

> George Eccles Dinosaur Park
> 1544 East Park Boulevard
> Ogden, UT 84401
> (801) 393-3466
> www.ogdencity.com

Moab Dinosaur Trails

The town of Moab, Utah, is located smack in the middle of some of the most spectacular country in North America. To the southwest are the seemingly endless gorges of Canyonlands National Park and to the northeast the graceful sandstone structures of Arches National Park. But for dino-hunters the prehistoric offerings near Moab are no less inspiring than the scenery.

Only a few miles to the north are several well-preserved dinosaur tracks. To the west of Highway 191 and just off Highway 279, are the tracks of a pair of theropods, likely meat-eaters, left in the red sandstone during the Early Jurassic. On the left of Highway 191, just past Mile Marker 141, is a trail leading to a whole series of tracks left by *Allosaurus*, *Stegosaurus*, and several other dinosaurs. Farther north on 191, just past Mile Marker 149, a trail leads to tracks made by heavy-footed sauropods. While footprints provide only indirect clues to the appearance of the animals that made them, they do offer something like a motion picture of the creature's way of life—how it moved, how fast, and why.

The trails mentioned above are relatively short, but can be rugged in places, and the tracks themselves can be difficult to

*M*ANY DINOSAURS *had striking headgear. For instance, the Cretaceous* Corythosaurus *had a wheel-shaped crest atop its head. The crest was mostly hollow with passages leading to its throat and the end of its snout. The crest might have served as an air horn, allowing the animal to signal other members of its herd when danger was near.*

The Late Cretaceous Parasaurolophus *had an even more striking crest sweeping back several feet behind its skull. Paleontologists once believed the elongated crest had served as a*

snorkel allowing the animal to feed for long periods underwater. This could not have been the case, however, since the crest had no hole at the end. Likely it functioned as a trumpet-like signaling device. With these amazing instruments on their heads Parasaurolophus *herds could have hooted warnings to one another from miles away.*

Both these duckbills were plant-eaters and grew to a length of about thirty feet. Their fossils are found at a variety of locations in western North America.

PARASAUROLOPHUS

find. Since the tracks are located on federal property, you will find it helpful to contact the Bureau of Land Management before your visit. You may enjoy your visit to the area more with the assistance of a guide. Information on tours, guides, transportation, and lodging can be found at the Web site listed below.

> Moab Dinosaur Trails
> Bureau of Land Management
> 82 East Dogwood
> Moab, UT 84532
> (435) 259-6111
> **www.moab.net**

Museum of San Raphael

Emery County, Utah, is right in the heart of dinosaur country and is the site of the well-known Cleveland-Lloyd Dinosaur Quarry. So it should come as no surprise that even the small Museum of San Raphael in the Emery county seat of Castle Dale has a fine assortment of dinosaur fossils. There is enough material here to make many museum curators from back east green with envy. The museum proudly displays a full-size *Allosaurus* skeleton and can boast excellent exhibits on ancient Indians.

Castle Dale visitors should take time out for a look at Goblin State Park in the San Raphael Swell area. This is the site of Robber's Roost, the notorious hideout of Butch Cassidy and his pal the Sundance Kid. The park takes its name from its weird limestone formations, and imaginative dino-hunters may be able to see the shapes of Jurassic creatures in the stone.

> Museum of San Raphael
> 64 North 100 East
> Castle Dale, UT 84513
> (435) 381-5252

Red Fleet State Park

Dinosaurs visited this area a long time before people came here. We know this because they left behind their footprints. At least two different species are thought to have made prints here. Modern human visitors can enjoy not only the prints, but also fishing, boating, and swimming.

> Red Fleet State Park
> 4335 North Highway 191
> Vernal, UT 84078
> (435) 789-4432
> www.nr.state.ut.us/parks/www1/redf.htm

Utah Field House of Natural History
Dinosaur Gardens

The Dinosaur Garden in Vernal is a delight with its full-size replica of *Tyrannosaurus rex*, *Triceratops*, *Coelophysis*, and more than a dozen other prehistoric beasts. The adjacent museum contains displays of fossilized skin and bone as well as an array of geology and archaeology exhibits.

> Utah Field House of Natural History
> Dinosaur Gardens
> 235 East Main
> Vernal, UT 84078
> (435) 789-3799
> www.utah.com

Utah Museum of Natural History

Located on the spacious 520-acre campus of the University of Utah in Salt Lake City, the Utah Museum of Natural Science rivals many of the nation's best-known museums in the size and quality of its collections. Over a million fossils, specimens, and artifacts are housed here. The Paleontology Hall will thrill dino-hunters with its full-size skeletal mounts of *Allosaurus*, *Camptosaurus*, and *Stegosaurus*. Also on display are fossil mammals such as the giant sloth, dire wolf, saber-toothed cat, and mammoth. A working paleontology laboratory allows visitors to watch paleontologists and trained volunteers clean dinosaur fossils and prepare them for exhibit.

Utah Museum of Natural History
University of Utah
1390 East Presidents Circle
Salt Lake City, UT 84112
(801) 581-6927
www.utah.edu

Weber State University Museum of Natural Science

After having a little fun with the replicas in Ogden's George Eccles Dinosaur Park (see page 216), dino-hunters may be in a mood to view some authentic fossils. The real thing can be found not too far away at the Natural Science Museum on the campus of Weber State University. In addition to a mounted skeleton of *Allosaurus*, there are skulls or fossils of *Apatosaurus*, *Camarasaurus*, *Camptosaurus*, *Dimetrodon*, and many other prehistoric creatures.

Weber State University Museum of Natural Science
Lind Lecture Hall
3750 Harrison Boulevard
Ogden, UT 84408
(801) 626-6653
catsis.weber.edu
www.ogdencity.com

Dinos in the
Upper Rockies

Hagerman Fossil Beds National Monument

The fabled Snake River has cut far down through the bluffs near Hagerman, Idaho, exposing sediments and fossils dating back some 3.5 million years. On a geological scale of time, these are relatively recent deposits, so there are no dinosaur bones to be found in them. However, there are plenty of fossils pointing to a modern animal almost as marvelous as the dinosaurs—namely, the horse. The Hagerman Fossil Beds contain one of the largest concentrations of horse fossils in the world, and they are significant in the study of equine evolution. The fossils found here are important also because they provide a glimpse at the Late Pliocene period just before the great Ice Ages began to sweep the planet. The modern flora and fauna we see today had already begun to appear by that time.

Established in 1988, the 4,280-acre Hagerman Fossil Beds National Monument is not heavily trafficked by the public. The visitors center in town provides interpretation of the fossils. The 150-year-old wagon ruts of the Oregon Trail run through the monument and provide an interesting contrast with the fossil beds, some twenty-three thousand times older.

Hagerman Fossil Beds National Monument
P.O. Box 570
Hagerman, ID 83332
(208) 837-4793
www.nps.gov/hafo

Idaho State Museum of Natural History

As is the case at the Hagerman Fossil Beds, most of the fossils collected in the state of Idaho date to the Pliocene, long after dinosaurs had disappeared. The locally gathered paleontology collections at the Idaho State Museum of Natural History in Pocatello are, therefore, rather light on dinosaur remains. However, extinct bison and other such Pliocene mammals are well represented. Overall, the museum can boast of 400,000 - plus specimens and artifacts. Of particular interest is the *Nature of Idaho* exhibit, which traces six hundred million years of evolution in this region through the local fossil record.

Idaho State Museum of Natural History
Idaho State University
P.O. Box 8096
Pocatello, ID 83209
(208) 236-3168
cwis.isu.edu/departments/museum

MONTANA

Carter County Museum

Among the Carter County Museum's displays of regionally important historic artifacts are some very interesting fossils.

Highlighting the collection are a Triceratops skull and a nearly complete skeleton of an *Anatosaurus*, known to most as a "duck-billed dinosaur."

Also in Carter County is Medicine Rocks State Park, where the weather has sculpted sandstone formations into fantastic shapes somehow suggestive of prehistoric times. With a little imagination you may see the figures of dinosaurs in them. Native American tribes once gathered in this area to pray and make "big medicine." Here they would call on the spirits of the wind, rain, and sky to help them during their buffalo hunts and guide them in their day-to-day lives.

Carter County Museum
100 Main Street
Ekalaka, MT 59324
(406) 775-6886
Medicine Rocks State Park
406-232-0900
www.ohwy.com/mt/e/ekalaka.htm

Garfield County Museum

Visitors will find here a *Tyrannosaurus rex* skull and a number of other fascinating fossils. But the star of the show at this small Jordan, Montana, museum is a full-size, mounted *Triceratops* dug out of a local hillside. While its dinosaur offerings are worthy and lots of fun, the museum devotes most of its exhibit space to Montana pioneer history. On the museum grounds are an authentic homestead cabin and an old blacksmith shop.

Garfield County Museum
P.O. Box 325
Jordon, MT 59318
(406) 557-2517
www.ohwy.com/mt/y/ygarfcom.htm

Museum of the Rockies/Paleo Field School

Like the wide-open Montana countryside spreading out in all directions from Bozeman, the 94,000-square-foot Museum of the Rockies has room enough to stretch your legs and your mind. This Montana State University facility offers a planetarium, living history farm, walking trail, picnic area, and enough exhibit and display space to guide visitors through more than four billion years of earth history.

The theme of the museum complex is "One Place Through All of Time," and this ambitious unifying concept is expressed in a myriad of ways. The Taylor Planetarium gets us started with a look at the Montana sky and a journey back to the beginning of time itself. A mural on the curved planetarium wall depicts the entire history of the universe from the "Big Bang" right down to the present day.

Much of the museum display area is devoted to "Landforms/ Lifeforms," a permanent exhibition offering a look at Montana's physical and natural development. Highlighted here are a time room, placing the slow geological changes into perspective, and the Early Earth Hall with its three beautiful dioramas illustrating life as it existed 520 million, 370 million, and 320 million years ago. A small theater gives visitors a glimpse of Pangaea, the supercontinent that encompassed much of the earth's dry land before the continents we know today began to drift apart.

Of course, dino-hunters will be anxious to get to the Dinosaur Hall with its "One Day 80 Million Years Ago" exhibition where they will find many fine fossils including an impressive *Triceratops* skull. There is also a delightful robotic mother *Triceratops* with her hatchlings. But the highlight of the exhibition is its display on *Maiasaura peeblesorum*, or "good mother lizard." Fossil findings have led paleontologists to believe this animal watchfully nurtured its young.

A LARGE CACHE of nests, eggs, and hatchlings discovered at a dig site in eastern Montana caused many paleontologists to reexamine their thinking on dinosaur behavior. The nests were evenly spaced and arranged in such a way that it seemed likely the mother dinosaurs had watched over and nurtured their young. The eggs had belonged to a type of hadrosaur, which was given the name Maiasaura, *or "Good Mother Lizard." Some of the nests contained the fossilized remains of baby dinosaurs.*

MAIASAURA

Among the other exhibit halls and galleries at this excellent museum are the Gardner Gallery, containing historic and prehistoric artifacts from the northern Rockies and plains, and the Paugh History Hall, providing a look at Montana in more recent times. The latter includes antique fire wagons, sleighs, buggies, stagecoaches, and many other such fascinating items.

Those who want to dig for dinosaurs themselves take note! The Museum of the Rockies and Montana State offer a Paleo Field School for aspiring paleontologists and enthusiastic amateurs. Guided by experts, students visit Montana digs and fossil quarries such as Egg Mountain. Field School courses of varying length provide insight into prehistory and an excellent grounding in the science of paleontology.

> Museum of the Rockies/Paleo Field School
> Montana State University
> 600 West Kagy Boulevard
> Bozeman, MT 59717
> (406) 994-2251
> www.montana.edu/wwwmon

Old Trail Museum

Located along the dramatic Front Range of the Rocky Mountains, the area around Choteau is rich not only in regional history but in fossils. The Old Trail Museum celebrates Choteau's heritage with fine displays of Native American and pioneer artifacts, but it also has on hand an abundance of fossils and dinosaur materials. Among the exhibits are three life-size skeletons including a mounted hadrosaur. Of particular interest to dino-hunters are the museum's field classes led by professional paleontologists. Lasting from two to ten days, the classes are available during warm-weather months and are great for both adults and children.

> Old Trail Museum
> 523 North Main Street
> Choteau, MT 59422
> (406) 466-5332
> www.ohwy.com/mt/c/choteau.htm

The Rock Shop

A private museum that sells locally quarried fossils and minerals, the Rock Shop is operated by a family of local paleontology buffs. Years ago, the owners discovered the remains of a juvenile dinosaur that turned out to be a rare *Maiasaura*, or "Good Mother Lizard." This is a great place to buy some fossils for your collection. Unlike the fossils you may—or may not—find out in the wilds, most of these will be carefully identified and labeled.

> The Rock Shop
> 161 South Front Street
> P.O. Box 796
> Bynum, MT 59419
> (406) 469-2314

Upper Musselshell Valley Museum

Local history is the primary focus of this small Montana museum, and it is filled with artifacts of pioneer life here in the Musselshell River Valley. The museum building is itself historic and dates to 1909. Dino-hunters will be fascinated by the casts of *Avaceratops* fossils found in this area during the early 1980s. The *Avaceratops* was a horned dinosaur not unlike the *Triceratops*, but smaller. Equally interesting is the museum's collection of duck-billed dinosaur remains.

> Upper Musselshell Valley Museum
> 11 South Central Avenue
> Harlowtown, MT 59036
> (406) 632-5519
> **www.ohwy.com/mt/u/upmussmu.htm**

NEVADA

Berlin Ichthyosaur State Park

Although the ichthyosaurs were seagoing reptiles and not true dinosaurs, they are a source of great fascination for dino-hunters. One of the best places in the world to see and study these wondrous creatures is the Berlin Ichthyosaur State Park in Nevada. Here paleontologists have uncovered the remains of nine of the big marine lizards, one almost thirty-five feet long. These are among the most complete and best-preserved ichthyosaurs yet discovered. Covered by a protective building, the fossils have been left partially exposed in their original configuration. This allows visitors to see the bones exactly as they were left on the bottom of the ocean long ago and to share with paleontologists the thrill of discovery.

Not to be missed at this Nevada State Park is the well-preserved ghost town of Berlin. Miners came here a century ago to dig mineral riches from the earth, rather than fossils.

Berlin Ichthyosaur State Park
HC 61, Box 61200
Austin, NV 89310
(775) 289-1636
www.nbmg.unr.edu/nl/nl21a.htm

Las Vegas Natural History Museum

One expects to see a good show in Las Vegas, and the desert city's Natural History Museum offers just that. The museum is devoted to wildlife past and present, so you will see plenty of dioramas and fossil exhibits here. You will also see wildlife art, animated dinosaurs, and even a tank filled with live sharks—well, this is Las Vegas after all. There are plenty of interactive exhibits to keep the kids happy.

Do not imagine that the Natural History Museum is the only place in Las Vegas to see dinosaurs. They pop up on neon signs, in hotels and casinos, and even on street corners. Chinatown Plaza offers a Jurassic Chinosaur exhibit—yes, that's

231

T HESE *"FISHLIKE LIZARDS"* grew to a length of fifty feet or more and roamed the earth's dark seas as long ago as 225 million years. Likely they fed on fish, hunting the shallow seas that spread across vast areas of the globe during the Jurassic. Since ichthyosaurs lacked gills, they must have bobbed to the surface at regular intervals to breathe. Some scientists believe they laid no eggs, but rather bore live young much as mammals do today.

ICHTHYOSAURS

right, Chinosaur—featuring nine full-size mounted skeletons or models along with excavation photographs, footprints, and assorted fossil specimens.

Las Vegas Natural History Museum
900 Las Vegas Boulevard North
Las Vegas, NV 89101
(702) 384-3466
www.vegaswebworld.com/lvnathistory

WYOMING

Bighorn Canyon National Recreation Area and Visitors Center

The heart of the seventy-thousand-acre Bighorn National Recreation Area is Bighorn Lake, a reservoir stretching across more than seventy miles of Montana and Wyoming range. There are two separate entrances, one near the town of Fort Smith in Montana and the other at Lovell, Wyoming. Interpretive trails provide information on the unique geology and prehistory of the region. The visitors center at Lovell has dinosaur and Cenozoic mammal fossils on display.

or

Bighorn Canyon National Recreation Area
P.O. Box 7458
Fort Smith, MT 59035
(406) 666-2412

Bighorn Canyon National Recreation Area/Visitors
Center
20 East Highway 14A
Lovell, WY 82431
(307) 548-2251
www.nps.gov/bica

Cody Dinosaur Quarries

Check with the Cody Chamber of Commerce concerning visits to some very productive dinosaur quarries in the northwestern corner of Wyoming. Cody is home of the Buffalo Bill Cody Historical Center and serves as the eastern gateway to Yellowstone National Park.

Cody Dinosaur Quarries
836 Sheridan
Cody, WY 82414
(307) 587-2777

233

Fossil Butte National Monument

About fifty million years ago a series of great lakes spread their waters across much of what are today the states of Colorado, Utah, and Wyoming. The lesser of these was Fossil Lake, a body of fresh water about fifty miles long and twenty miles wide. This warm, Cenozoic lake teemed with life. Gars, bowfins, paddlefish, herring, perch, crocodiles, turtles, rays, and dozens of other species swam in its clear waters. A lush forest made up of oaks, maples, beeches, and many other trees and shrubs familiar to us today grew along its banks.

Time has turned this scene upside down and replaced the region's once-moist climate with near-desert conditions. Rugged Buttes have now thrust the bottom of Fossil Lake high into the air. Its remnants consist of a layer of tan sedimentary rock called the Green River Formation. For almost a century paleontologists have sifted through the formation in search of early Cenozoic fossils, and their finds are now exhibited in museums throughout the world.

One of the most productive fossil quarries is located a little more than a mile from the visitors center at Fossil Butte National Monument near Kemmerer, Wyoming. Established in 1972 to preserve this rich prehistoric resource, the monument provides public access to many of its wonders. Trails lead to key quarry sites and offer ample opportunity to study existing flora and fauna.

Since the Green River Formation was laid down well after the end of the Cretaceous, there are no dinosaurs here. Even so, paleontology buffs and rock hounds will find this place hard to resist. The visitors center has a thirteen-foot Fossil Lake crocodile on display as well as early bat remains and a mass of fish fossils—apparently the fish seen in this exhibit died together in some mysterious calamity. The trails are spectacular, but visitors are reminded not to disturb or remove rocks and fossils.

Fossil Butte National Monument
P.O. Box 592
Kemmerer, WY 83101
(307) 877-4455
www.nps.gov/fobu

Greybull Museum

In 1934, a Wyoming cowboy made an astonishing discovery on his ranch near the little town of Greybull. He found some bones that were way too big to be those of cattle, bison, or anything else he had ever seen. They were, in fact, dinosaur fossils. News of the find reached the ears of collectors in the East, and before the year was out they had removed thirty railcar loads of fossils from a quarry on the ranch. Many of these were shipped to the American Museum of Natural History in New York, but some eventually ended up in the modest but worthy Greybull museum. Dino-hunters on safari in Wyoming should not miss them.

Greybull Museum
325 Greybull Street
Greybull, WY 82462
(307) 765-2444

Sheridan College Geology Museum

The geology department of this small Wyoming college operates its own dinosaur quarry in Johnson County, Wyoming. Here faculty and students explore an exposed section of the fossil-rich Morrison Formation. Much of what they unearth here ends up in the campus geology museum. Among the prize fossils they have recovered is part of a twenty-five-foot-long *Allosaurus* skeleton. They have also uncovered a considerable quantity of *Camarasaurus* and other sauropod specimens.

Sheridan College Geology Museum
P.O. Box 1500
Sheridan, WY 82801
(307) 674-6446
www.sc.whecn.edu

Tate Mineralogical Museum

The three slashing claws of the *Wyomingraptor* on display at the Tate Mineralogical Museum in Casper look like something out of a bad science fiction movie. Apparently, this *Allosaurus*-type, Late Jurassic predator was well armed. So, too, were some of the other meat-eating dinos featured at this museum located on the Casper College campus. The gaping jaws of the Tate's prize *Tyrannosaurus* skull were formidable enough to bite off half a ton of meat at a time. This *T-rex* has been nicknamed "Stan" and is something of a Tate Museum mascot. Also on exhibit is a bony flipper from a 150-million-year-old marine reptile. The flipper was at least five feet long, so this predatory creature was a true sea monster—an oceangoing version of "Stan."

In addition to a helpful on-line tour of the museum with photos of some of its key paleontology exhibits, the Tate Web site features a "Mesozoic Picture Gallery." Included are a dozen pieces of dino-art by Bob Bakker. You'll see a fighting *Iguanodon*, a leaping *Deinonychus*, a feeding *Megalosaurus*, and much more.

Tate Mineralogical Museum
Casper College
125 College Drive
Casper, WY 82601
(307) 268-2447
www.cc.whecn.edu/tate/webpage.htm

University of Wyoming Geological Museum

The main hall of the Geology Museum at the University of Wyoming contains a number of spectacular mounted skeletons. Among them is a cast of "Big Al," a twenty-five-foot-long young adult *Allosaurus* who was a lot more lively 150 million years ago than he is nowadays. His skeleton was found on public land in 1991 and painstakingly removed by teams from the Museum of the Rockies and the University of Wyoming. Big Al's skeleton is particularly interesting since it reveals a number of skeletal injuries ranging from broken ribs to crushed fingers. The animal must have lived a hard life.

Accompanying Big Al is a seventy-five-foot-long *Apatosaurus*, which probably weighed about twenty-five tons when it was alive during the Jurassic. Overhead, a Late Cretaceous *Pteranodon* is suspended in air, its wings extended. The *Pteranodon* had an elongated skull with a shovel beak allowing it to scoop up fish much as pelicans do today. Also featured are a seven-foot-long *Triceratops* skull and a huge *Tyrannosaurus* skull with bared teeth. Outside a two-story *T-rex* model greets museum visitors.

Serious dino-hunters should note: During summers, field expeditions are jointly offered by the University of Wyoming Geology Museum and the Museum of the Rockies at Montana State University. Dinosaur enthusiasts are allowed to dig for fossils alongside expert paleontologists. Team members must be age fifteen or older. Space is limited, so make arrangements well in advance.

University of Wyoming Geological Museum
P.O. Box 3006
Laramie, WY 82071
(307) 766-4218
(307) 766-2646 (for dinosaur digs)
www.uwyo.edu/geomuseum

*M*ANY OF *us have grown up knowing this giant sauropod by the name* Brontosaurus. *In 1877, schoolteacher Arthur Lakes discovered several huge fossil bones near Morrison, Colorado. Lakes sold his find to a Yale professor, the bone warrior O. C. Marsh, who described the fossils as belonging to an animal he named* Apatosaurus *("Deceptive Lizard"). Two years later Marsh gave the name* Brontosaurus *("Thunder Lizard") to a second set of fossils found in Wyoming. It would eventually be shown that the* Apatosaurus *and* Brontosaurus *were the same creature. Even so, the name* Brontosaurus *stuck for many years, perhaps because of the dramatic image it evoked—that of an animal so large that it shook the earth when it moved. Much later paleontologists would honor scientific tradition by reverting to the earlier name.*

Tradition or no, "Thunder Lizard" would not have been a bad name for the Apatosaurus. *At seventy feet in length from head to tail and weighing up to thirty tons, it was a very big dinosaur*

APATOSAURUS

indeed. It had stout elephant-like legs and padded feet to support its tremendous bulk. The evidence provided by trackways suggests that these enormous Jurassic plant-eaters traveled considerable distances in herds, perhaps in search of better grazing. It is easy to imagine that a herd of Apatosaurus *generated something like a minor earthquake when it moved.*

Western Wyoming Community College Museum

The museum at this small Wyoming college has a number of interesting fossils on display as well as several dinosaur models. The college offers an excellent archaeology program with a working field school, so much of what you'll see here pertains to human prehistory.

> Western Wyoming Community College Museum
> 2500 College Drive
> Rock Springs, WY 82901
> (307) 382-1600
> www.wwcc.cc.wy.us

Wyoming State Museum

Not necessarily the best place in Wyoming to study fossils and dinosaurs, the State Museum in Cheyenne offers only a few scattered prehistory exhibits. However, you may want to see the big mammoth tooth on display here. Also, the museum staff can offer helpful advice if you plan to hunt dinos elsewhere in this ruggedly beautiful state.

> Wyoming State Museum
> Barret Building
> 2301 Central Avenue
> Cheyenne, WY 82002
> (307) 777-7022

Dinos in the
Far West

Dorthy G. Page Museum

One might not expect to find an important dinosaur fossil in a far-off corner of Alaska, but Wasilla's Page Museum holds a rare and much sought after *Nodosaurus* skull. Its back protected by a covering of thick armor plates, the *Nodosaurus* looked much like an armadillo, albeit an enormous one—up to eighteen feet long. Given to the museum by a local donor, the skull is coveted by institutions such as the University of Alaska Museum in Fairbanks and the Smithsonian in Washington. It may eventually be given up to a larger museum, but for the moment it remains in Wasilla.

> Dorthy G. Page Museum
> Page Museum
> 323 Main Street
> Wasilla, AK 99654
> (907) 373-9071

University of Alaska Museum

Visitors walking into the University of Alaska Museum in Fairbanks cannot help but be impressed by the nine-foot-tall brown bear that greets them. This mounted specimen is harmless enough, but those who have met up with a live brown bear in the wild may think they've seen the modern equivalent of *Tyrannosaurus rex*.

The broad galleries beyond the big bear include displays on Alaska geological history, ethnology, wildlife, and a host of other subjects related to the Great Land of the North. Those in search of dinosaurs here will find them. The museum's Western and Arctic Coast Gallery includes an outstanding exhibit on dinosaurs of Alaska. Most fossils were taken from Alaska's North Slope region and date to the Cretaceous period. For dinohunters, this extensive collection raises the question of just what dinosaurs were doing in such high and chilly latitudes.

University of Alaska Museum
907 Yukon Drive
P.O. Box 756960
Fairbanks, AK 99775
(907) 474-7505
www.uaf.edu/museum

CALIFORNIA

Anza Borrego Desert State Park

Stretching across 600,000 spectacular acres of southern California, this is the largest state park in the continental United States. It encompasses two separate wilderness areas, several verdant canyons, and numerous oases and cactus gardens. The park offers five hundred miles of rugged dirt roads and many miles more of hiking trails leading visitors to scenic wonders they may never have imagined.

Fossils are abundant in this desert park, and visitors are encouraged to study and learn from them. What the dino-hunter won't find here are—well—dinosaurs. Most of the land in the park is of much too recent formation, dating back only a few million years into the Pliocene. That means the park's fossils are primarily those of mammals and sea creatures who lived in fairly recent times—by dinosaur standards. Still the Anza Borrego Park is a treasure offering a sense of what the earth was like during all those eons before the arrival of humanity.

> Anza Borrego Desert State Park
> Borrego Springs, CA 92004
> (760) 767-5311
> **www.anzaborrego.statepark.org**

Dinny

This roadside *Apatosaurus* is a favorite of travelers zooming along through the California desert on I-10. A rather fanciful creation, such as one might expect to see in southern California, he is known to one and all as "Dinny." About 150 feet long, he dates to the early 1960s when he was fashioned from scrap materials and more than a thousand bags of cement. In Dinny's ample belly is—you guessed it—a gift shop.

> "Dinny" Museum and Shop
> P.O. Box 231
> Cabazon, CA 92230
> (909) 849-8309

Jurupa Mountain Cultural Center

Dino-hunting adults and children will find plenty to like about this unique learning facility. Located in the hills above Riverside, California, the Jurupa Mountain Cultural Center offers a variety of paleontology-and-dinosaur-related activities including fossil collection and identification. You know you're in the right place when you see the eight giant dinosaur replicas arrayed on the hillside behind the museum. There are some nice fossil, rock, mineral, and gem displays inside the museum, but the best stuff is waiting outside. Depending on the day and the field trip you choose, the center's guides will invite you to pan for gold, collect geological specimens, polish rocks, grow plants from cuttings, and even make Native American pictographs. The fossil-collecting field trips are especially attractive for kids.

> Jurupa Mountain Cultural Center
> 7621 Granite Hill Drive
> Riverside, CA 92509
> (909) 685-5818
> **www.dreamsoft.com/home.htm**

La Brea Tar Pits

The focus here is on the Ice Age not the Age of Dinosaurs, but your experience at La Brea will be nonetheless thrilling. Between ten thousand and forty thousand years ago, mammoths, saber-toothed cats, giant sloths, and a host of other creatures became ensnared in the asphaltlike tars of the La Brea Pits. Their tar-covered bones have yielded a treasure trove of information about life in the Los Angeles Basin during the last Ice Age. Today a park and museum celebrate the contributions of these tar pits to paleontology.

Originally part of the Rancho La Brea, a historic Mexican land grant, the pits were once mined for their natural asphalt. Later they would be mined instead for their valuable fossils. Many of the skeletons recovered from the pits are on display at the Page Museum adjacent to the tar pits. An extension of the much larger Los Angeles Museum of Natural History, the Page Museum is surrounded by the twenty-three-acre Hancock Park featuring observation pits, life-size replicas of extinct animals, and plants that were present here during the Ice Age.

La Brea Tar Pits
George C. Page Museum
5801 Wilshire Boulevard
Los Angeles, CA 90036
(323) 934-7243
www.tarpits.org

Museums at Blackhawk

In Danville, to the east of San Francisco and Oakland, is a unique complex known as the Museums at Blackhawk. Founded originally as an automotive museum, this highly educational and entertaining facility also includes separate anthropology and paleontology museums. The first-rate prehistory displays here include fossils, skulls, or articulated skeletons of *Allosaurus*, *Dilophosaurus*, *Ichthyosaurus*, and *Phytosaurus*, an early crocodile.

Museums at Blackhawk
3700 Blackhawk Plaza Circle
Danville, CA 94506
(510) 736-2277
www.blackhawkauto.org

Petrified Forest

The huge petrified logs found here date back about three million years, so the dinosaurs were long gone by the time these trees were felled by some cataclysm—likely a volcanic eruption. Their age is only a tiny fraction of the age of the 225-million-year-old trees in Arizona's Petrified Forest National Park. Still, these giants are well worth seeing as they illustrate the processes by which nature turns once-living matter into fossils. The big stone logs

*S*EVERAL TYPES *of large cat roamed the Ice Age landscape. Some had formidable canine teeth up to several inches long. Many saber-toothed cat skeletons have been found at the La Brea Tar Pits in southern California and at other such Ice Age fossil caches. Presumably, the big cats came to the pits to prey on animals that had gotten stuck in the tar, and then became trapped themselves. With their menacing fangs, the skulls make dramatic museum displays.*

SABER-TOOTHED CAT

were first excavated about 1871 by a Swedish immigrant whose fascination with them earned him the nickname "Petrified Charlie." The forest has remained in private hands through the years and is now operated as a museum and tourist attraction.

Petrified Forest
4100 Petrified Forest Road
Calistoga, CA 94515
(707) 942-6667
www.petrifiedforest.org

San Bernadino County Museum

This Redlands museum proudly displays a significant number of prized fossils. Of primary interest, however, are the nearby

*T*HE NODOSAURUS *was built a bit like a modern armadillo, except that it was very much larger—in fact, bigger than most automobiles. Thick, bony plates protected the upper half of its eighteen-foot-long body. In this way the* Nodosaurus *was similar to the* Ankylosaurus. *Predators would have had a hard time getting around or biting through the* Nodosaurus's *armor. Fossils of this dinosaur are quite rare, and for this reason, it remains poorly known.*

NODOSAURUS

dinosaur trackways, the only ones ever found in California. Museum staff and volunteers lead regular field trips to the site of the tracks, left here millions of years ago by creatures now vanished into air, rock, and time itself.

San Bernadino County Museum
2024 Orange Tree Lane
Redlands, CA 92374
(909) 307-2669

San Diego Museum of Natural History

One of the oldest scientific institutions in the West, the San Diego Museum of Natural History has been gathering fossil specimens and artifacts for the better part of a century. Today the museum is a favorite attraction of popular Balboa Park. Dino-hunters will be fascinated by the museum's *Allosaurus* and other articulated dinosaur skeletons. A special museum feature is its rare *Nodosaurus,* the only known remains of this large armored creature ever found in the far West.

San Diego was, of course, the site of a key scene in the Michael Creighton–Steven Speilberg dinosaur potboiler *The Lost World.* Therein, an out-of-its-era and understandably angry *Tyrannosaurus rex* rampages through San Diego, demolishing filling stations, terrorizing motorists, and chewing on traffic signals. All this is great fun even if it is also 190-proof fiction. No doubt, the movie increased museum visitation dramatically.

> San Diego Museum of Natural History
> 1788 El Prado
> P.O. Box 1390
> San Diego, CA 92112
> (619) 232-3821
> www.sdnhm.org

Santa Barbara Museum of Natural History

Anyone interested in marine biology will find the Santa Barbara Museum of Natural History particularly enjoyable. The fossil displays are worth seeing, but the big attraction here is the Marine Hall where an enormous whale skeleton impresses with its sheer size. Some modern whales are, after all, bigger than the largest of the dinosaurs.

The handsome dioramas in the Mammal Hall are a must-see. So, too, are the exhibits on the wildlife of the rugged Santa Barbara Channel Islands. Don't miss the dwarf mammoth skeleton in the Paleontology Hall. The very term "dwarf mammoth" would seem an oxymoron, but nature created this oddity when a herd of woolly mammoths became stranded on one of California's Channel Islands at the end of the last Ice Age. The meager food supplies on the island made it difficult for the huge mammoths to sustain their bulky frames. Even so, these creatures survived for many generations after larger mammoths on the mainland had passed into extinction. They managed this by evolving, through the process of natural selection, a diminished and almost toylike stature. Anyone who has doubts about evolution and how it works should have a look at this little mammoth.

> Santa Barbara Museum of Natural History
> 2559 Puesta del Sol Road
> Santa Barbara, CA 93105
> (805) 682-4711
> www.sbnature.org

Skullduggery

Not a museum or public institution, but rather a private business, Skullduggery produces and sells museum-quality fossil replicas. Since true fossils are delicate and should be left mostly in the experienced hands of scientists, these first-rate reproductions have much to offer collectors. The fascinating showroom is open to the public. Skullduggery maintains a first-rate Web site and an on-line catalog.

> Skullduggery
> 624 South B Street
> Tustin, CA 92780
> (800) 336-7745
> www.skullduggery.com

University of California Museum of Paleontology

Although primarily a research institution, the Museum of Paleontology maintains a number of fine fossil exhibits in the Valley Life Sciences Building on the Berkeley campus. Among them are a fully mounted *Tyrannosaurus rex* ferocious enough

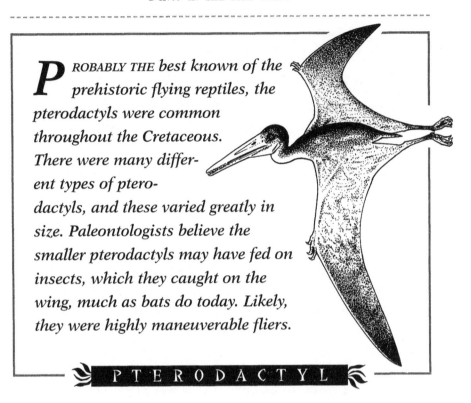

*P*ROBABLY THE *best known of the prehistoric flying reptiles, the pterodactyls were common throughout the Cretaceous. There were many different types of pterodactyls, and these varied greatly in size. Paleontologists believe the smaller pterodactyls may have fed on insects, which they caught on the wing, much as bats do today. Likely, they were highly maneuverable fliers.*

PTERODACTYL

to scare the daylights out of even the most jaded visitor. There is also a mounted *Pteranodon ingens* as well as massive skulls of *Triceratops* and *Edmontosaurus* and equally impressive exhibits on *Archaeopteryx, Parasaurolophus, Phytosaurus, Ichthysaurus,* and *Heterodontosaurus* (a small, Late Jurassic herbivore), and many other species. For the benefit of those who can't visit the Oakland-Berkeley area at the moment, the staff maintains a "Virtual Museum of Paleontology," accessible on the Internet at the address listed below.

University of California Museum of Paleontology
University of California
Berkeley, CA 94720
(510) 642-1821
www.ucmp.berkeley.edu/exhibit/exhibits.html

OREGON

John Day Fossil Beds National Monument

For many millions of years plants and animals thrived in what are now known as the John Day Fossil Beds. What is today a rugged and inhospitable stretch of rugged badlands was then a subtropical forest alive with amphibians, reptiles, mammals, and lush greenery. These living things left a record of their existence in a thick fossil deposit now underlying the badlands. It was created by layers of ash laid down one after another by repeated volcanic eruptions.

The fossil record here covers a period of approximately forty-five million years spanning much of the Cenozoic period. Since the dinosaurs were gone by the time the Cenozoic began, you won't find their bones among these fossils. However, anyone with an interest in paleontology will love this place.

In 1974 Congress protected this extraordinary scientific resource through the creation of the John Day Fossil Beds National Monument. Encompassing a total of fourteen thousand acres, it is broken into three separate units: Clarno, Painted Hills, and Sheep Rock. The latter contains the monument headquarters and visitors center where you will find excellent fossil displays. In each of the units trails lead through rich fossil beds to breathtaking vistas. Keep in mind that removing or disturbing the fossils is strictly forbidden.

John Day Fossil Beds National Monument
HCR Box 126
Kimberly, OR 97848
(541) 987-2333
www.nps.gov/joda

T H. HUXLEY, *a Victorian-era scientist and early dino-hunter, was among the first to recognize the similarities between dinosaur skeletons and those of modern birds and did so while he was carving a Christmas turkey. Holding a drumstick in his hand, he gazed at the fleshless carcass and wondered whether birds were descended from some type of dinosaur. Evidence that this might be the case emerged as early as 1869. That year, an extraordinary fossilized skeleton was found in a German quarry. The delicate bones of this small creature—now known as* Archaeopteryx—*were accompanied by the clear impressions of feathers. Birds are the only animals known to have feathers, and yet the* Archaeopteryx *had many skeletal features in common with dinosaurs. The link was hard to dismiss.*

While the theory remains controversial, it has gained wider acceptance recently. The Late Jurassic Archaeopteryx *that helped spark the controversy was apparently a tree dweller and used its feathered wings for gliding, perhaps to escape predators. Ironically, many paleontologists now believe that the* Archaeopteryx *was probably not a direct ancestor of birds, but rather one of many evolutionary dead ends along the path that led eventually to eagles, parakeets, pigeons, and even—turkeys.*

ARCHAEOPTERYX

❧ ELASMOSAURUS ❧

*T*HE LATE CRETACEOUS *oceans were patrolled by the* Elasmosaurus, *a predatory marine reptile of tremendous size. A type of plesiosaur, it had a pronounced neck, taking up more than half its forty-five-foot length. Likely, its long neck gave the* Elasmosaurus *greater striking range when hunting.*

Prehistoric Gardens

A walk through the coastal Oregon rain forest with its giant trees and ferns may very well convince you that you have gone back in time to the Jurassic period. Close your eyes and you can imagine a herd of dinosaurs rumbling past. At the Prehistoric Gardens in Port Orford, you can keep your eyes open and imagine the same thing. Nearly two dozen dinosaur models inhabit the rain forest here. You may not learn much science when you visit, but you *will* have a lot of fun.

Prehistoric Gardens
36848 Highway 101 South
Port Orford, OR 97465
(541) 332-4463

Washington

Burke Museum of Natural History and Culture

Natural history exhibits at the Burke Museum, located on the University of Washington campus in Seattle, tell the story of Washington's often-violent prehistory. Even recent geological developments in Washington have been action-packed. Remember Mount Saint Helens? But so, too, was the remote prehistory of this state, forged in the fires of colliding continental plates and erupting volcanoes.

The museum's paleontology collection includes nearly three million specimens, so there is plenty of dinosaur stuff here—most of it, unfortunately, is not on display. Even so, dino-hunters will find a lot to like at the Burke. The *Dino Times* exhibition shows off a number of fine mounted skeletons such as a *Stegosaurus*, an *Elasmosaurus*, and a 140-million-year-old *Allosaurus*. The "Cold Times" exhibition filled with—you guessed it—Ice Age materials, boasts a ten thousand-year old mastodon skeleton, a saber-toothed cat, and a giant ground sloth accidentally dug up and then rescued from an airport construction site.

> Burke Museum of Natural History and Culture
> Box 353010
> University of Washington
> Seattle, WA 98195
> (206) 543-5590
> www.washington.edu/burkemuseum

Ginko Petrified Forest State Park

During the 1930s, highway construction crews uncovered a large cache of petrified wood in the Columbia River Gorge near Vantage, Washington. Much of the fossilized wood turned out to be that of an extinct North American cousin of the Asian ginko tree. Trails through the 7,500-acre Ginko Petrified Forest State Park provide close-up views of the fifteen-million-year-old wood. Incidentally, the lovely ginko is now extinct throughout the world in the wild, but still survives as a specimen tree.

Ginko Petrified Forest State Park
40380 Old Vantage Highway
Vantage, WA 98950
(509) 856-2710
(800) 233-0321
www.parks.wa.gov

Dinos in
Canada

Provincial Museum of Alberta

The curators at Alberta's Provincial Museum in Edmonton had forty thousand square feet of exhibit space to work with, and they filled it with a mind-expanding array of dioramas and specimens. Visitors get sweeping views of both the past and present in this beautiful province with its wide-open plains and rugged mountains. The Natural History Gallery explores the prehistory of the region with displays of rocks, gems, and fossils and some spectacular mounted skeletons and models. Among the latter are an *Albertosaurus*—naturally enough—*Corythosaurus*, *Ankylosaurus*, saber-toothed cat, Irish elk, mammoth, and many other fine pieces. The museum Web site offers several fascinating on-line tours, but they are not necessarily related to dinosaurs.

> Provincial Museum of Alberta
> 12845 102d Avenue
> Edmonton, Alberta, Canada T5N 0M6
> (780) 453-9100
> **www.pma.edmonton.ab.ca**

BRITISH COLUMBIA

Courtenay Museum

British Columbia's huge Vancouver Island is rich in fossils, although they are not necessarily Canadian in origin. The island was once located off the coast of Baja California, arriving at its present position only after about eighty million years of continental drift. Many of the fossils found here are of marine reptiles—not dinosaurs—although they date to Mesozoic times. Excellent displays of these sea monsters can be seen at the Courtenay Museum and Paleontology Centre. You'll find more than five thousand fossils here including remains of elasmosaurs and mosasaurs. The museum organizes tours of local fossil excavation sites.

> Courtenay Museum
> 360 Cliffe Avenue
> Courtenay, British Columbia, Canada V9N 2H9
> (250) 334-3611
> **www.courtenaymuseum.bc.ca**

Yoho National Park

Canada can boast of some of the oldest rocks on earth, and not a few of these can be found in beautiful Yoho National Park in the mountains of British Columbia. In 1909, famed paleontologist Charles Walcott went for a walk in the Canadian Rockies and, near the top of Burgess Pass, stumbled across a fossil cache of extraordinary age. They were the remains of soft-bodied marine invertebrates as many as half a billion years old. Over the years since, several fossil quarries in or near Yoho Park have been worked and most have yielded stunning discoveries. Some of these can be seen at the Yoho Information Center in Field. The park offers tours of some quarry sites.

Yoho National Park
Box 99
Field, British Columbia, Canada V0A 1G0
(250) 343-6783
www.worldweb.com/ParksCanada-Yoho

MANITOBA

Manitoba Museum of Man and Nature

Part of an educational complex in Winnipeg featuring a science center and planetarium as well as an exhibit building, the Museum of Man and Nature celebrates the natural and human heritage of the giant mid-continent province of Manitoba. The museum conserves upward of 1.8 million humanities artifacts and about 120,000 natural science specimens, only a fraction of which are on display. Since Manitoba was underwater throughout much of prehistory, most of the collection is devoted to marine fossils. However, there are some dinosaur materials, most of them excavated in Alberta.

Manitoba Museum of Man and Nature
190 Rupert Avenue
Winnipeg, Manitoba, Canada R3B 0N2
(204) 956-2830
www.manitobamuseum.mb.ca

Morden Museum

A small Manitoba prairie town best known for its Corn and Apple Festival, Morden has a surprise in store for paleontology buffs. There is a nice little museum here featuring an abundance

T HIS LARGE *carnosaur is named for the Canadian
province of Alberta where it was discovered. A
Late Cretaceous hunter, it looked and, no doubt,
behaved much like the larger and better known*
Tyrannosaurus rex.

ALBERTOSAURUS

of marine fossils. They date back to the Cretaceous, a time when
shallow seas covered much of Manitoba. Highlighted here are
mounted skeletons of a plesiosaur, ichthyosaur, and mosasaur.

> Morden Museum
> 111 B Gilmore
> Morden, Manitoba, Canada R6M 1N9
> (204) 822-3406
> www.cici.mb.ca/dwood2/morden.html

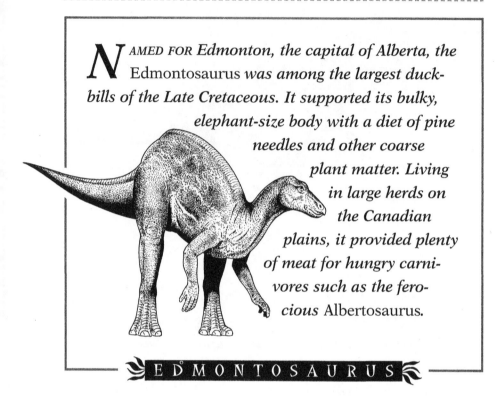

*N*AMED FOR *Edmonton, the capital of Alberta, the* Edmontosaurus *was among the largest duck-bills of the Late Cretaceous. It supported its bulky, elephant-size body with a diet of pine needles and other coarse plant matter. Living in large herds on the Canadian plains, it provided plenty of meat for hungry carnivores such as the ferocious* Albertosaurus.

E D M O N T O S A U R U S

NOVA SCOTIA

Nova Scotia Museum

The scenic Nova Scotia coast is surely among the few places on earth where dinosaur fossils are found among the driftwood and shells by the tide. The rugged shores of this province are composed of rocks dating to the Mesozoic era, the Age of Dinosaurs. More than a few of the fossils discovered here have found their way into the Nova Scotia Museum of Natural History in Halifax. Some are very old indeed, as much as one hundred million years older than the Morrison Formation that contains fossils of Cretaceous creatures such as *Tyrannosaurus rex.* The museum contains several life-size reconstructions including a very impressive pilot whale skeleton.

> Nova Scotia Museum
> 1747 Summer Street
> Halifax, Nova Scotia, Canada B3H 3A6
> (902) 424-6471
> **www.ednet.ns.ca/educ/museum**

QUEBEC

Parc de Miguasha

The fossils found here are very old, and they predate the dinosaurs. In fact, there were not yet any vertebrates on land 370 million years ago when lakes and inlets then covering this area were filled with primitive fishes. The exposed fossils in the Devonian cliffs in this park may provide insight into that mysterious era when living things first crawled up out of the sea.

> Parc de Miguasha
> 270 Route Miguasha Ouest
> Nouvelle, Quebec, Canada G0C 2E0
> (418) 794-2475
> **www.mef.gouv.qc.ca**

Redpath Museum

Housed in one of the oldest museum buildings in Canada, the Redpath has a classical look suggestive of the Roman Forum. It was built in 1882 to preserve and display the collections of a single man, noted naturalist Sir William Dawson. Since then the museum's collections have grown to encompass mineralogy, paleontology, ornithology, mammology, invertebrate zoology, ethnology, and archaeology. A relatively small facility, the

Redpath is used primarily as a research and teaching resource for McGill University, but is open to the public on a limited basis. Visitors should check first with the university for hours and accessibility, but it is worth the effort. Those who come will see some excellent mounted skeletons including *Albertosaurus*, *Coelophysis*, *Dromaeosaurus*, *Ichthyosaurus*, *Plesiosaurus*, and *Teleosaurus* (a Jurassic crocodile).

> Redpath Museum
> McGill University
> 859 Sherbrooke West
> Montreal, Quebec, Canada H3A 2K6
> (514) 398-4086
> **www.mcgill.ca/Redpath**

SASKATCHEWAN

Royal Saskatchewan Museum

The moving *T-rex* model at the Royal Saskatchewan Museum is such a favorite that local children have given it the nickname "Megamunch." Actually, the model is a stand-in for "Scotty" a scientifically important *Tyrannosaurus* skeleton being excavated by museum experts at a dig site near Eastend, Saskatchewan. The same dinosaur quarry has produced fossils of *Triceratops*, *Edmontosaurus*, *Thescelosaurus* (a Late Cretaceous bird-hipped plant-eater), *Chirostenotes* (a small, Late Cretaceous theropod), and *Saurornitholestes* (another lightly built Cretaceous theropod). Many of the fossils recovered here are now on display at the museum in the provincial capital of Regina.

Museum exhibits take visitors through hundreds of millions of years of Saskatchewan natural history including the Age of the Dinosaurs and at least five major glacial ages. In addition to the dinos, you'll want to see the 94-million-year-old crocodile, 70-million-year old plesiosaur, and 73-million-year-old mosasaur. An impressive new science gallery is scheduled to open in 2000.

> Royal Saskatchewan Museum
> 2445 Albert Street
> Regina, Saskatchewan, Canada S4P 3V7
> (306) 787-2815
> **www.saskweb.com/~tregina/rsm.html**

University of Saskatchewan Museum of Natural Sciences

The University of Saskatchewan in Saskatoon keeps a number of dinosaur and flying reptile replicas on display in its natural sciences and geology museum.

> University of Saskatchewan Museum of
> Natural Sciences
> Department of Geological Sciences
> University of Saskatchewan
> Saskatoon, Saskatchewan, Canada S7N 5E2
> (306) 966-5683
> **www.usask.ca/geology**

Digging for

If you are anxious to get your hands dirty digging for clues to the past, you'll find plenty of opportunities. Many natural history museums offer classes, travel programs, day-digs, or extended expeditions that allow ordinary folks like us to participate in the great adventure of paleontology. Check with the education departments of museums in your state or region for schedules and other information. Or try one or more of the parks, museums, or organizations below.

Aurora Fossil Museum

Tailings from mines near this small North Carolina museum often contain shark teeth, whale bone, shells, and coral from prehistoric seas. Visitors may sort through piles of tailings and keep any fossils they find.

> Aurora Fossil Museum
> 400 Main Street
> P.O. Box 352
> Aurora, NC 27806
> (252) 322-4238

Calvert Cliffs State Park

While they won't find dinosaur bones here, paleontology fans can dig for shark teeth and other Miocene marine fossils. Even better, they can keep what they find.

Calvert Cliffs State Park
Point Lookout State Park
P.O. Box 48
Scotland, MD 20687
(301) 872-5688

Caesar Creek Lake

The bad news is there are no dinosaur fossils here. The good news is there are plenty of shark teeth, trilobites, and other marine fossils—and U.S. Army Corps of Engineers will let you keep a few of them.

Caesar Creek Lake
U.S. Army Corps of Engineers
4020 North Clarksville
Waynesville, OH 45068
(513) 897-1050

Cincinnati Museum of Natural History

The museum's field expeditions are open to amateurs willing to share the costs. This excellent program provides direct experience in paleontology fieldwork while allowing participants to help advance the cause of science.

Cincinnati Museum of Natural History
1301 Western Avenue
Cincinnati, OH 45203
(513) 287-7000

Denver Museum of Natural History

The museum's on-site certification program for field and lab work is an outstanding opportunity for anyone seriously interested in paleontology. Taught by curators and associates, courses are open to adults age seventeen and up.

> Denver Museum of Natural History
> 2001 Colorado Boulevard
> Denver, CO 80205
> (800) 925-2250
> (303) 370-6303 (for courses)

Dinosaur Discovery Museum

Located in fossil-rich western Colorado, the museum organizes exciting five-day expeditions with time spent in the classroom, the laboratory, and the field. Professional paleontologists lead the digs.

> Dinosaur Discovery Museum
> Dinosaur Discovery Expeditions
> 550 Jurassic Court
> Fruita, CO 81521
> (800) DIG-DINO

Dinosaur State Park

Dinosaur tracks can be just as revealing as fossil bones. At this Connecticut state park visitors can make their own casting of a dinosaur footprint.

> Dinosaur State Park
> West Street
> Rocky Hill, CT 06067
> (860) 529-8423

Dinosaur Valley Museum

Dinosaur Valley offers both "Day Digs" and "Major Expeditions" allowing amateurs to help gather real dinosaur fossils. Here's a great place to add some bonus points to your dino-score.

> Dinosaur Valley Museum
> 362 West Main Street
> P.O. Box 20000
> Grand Junction, CO 81502
> (970) 241-9210 or (888) 488-DINO

Fort Worth Museum of Science and History

The museum maintains a special exhibit called "DinoDig" where visitors can dig for casts of *Tenontosaurus* fossils. A replica of a real Texas fossil quarry, the exhibit provides true-to-life and scientifically accurate field paleontology experiences.

> Fort Worth Museum of Science and History
> 1501 Montgomery Street
> Fort Worth, TX 76107
> (817) 732-1631

Garden Park Paleontology Society

The society makes its home in Canon City, Colorado, near the site of one the oldest dinosaur quarries in North America. An educational center operated by the society offers training in paleontology field- and lab work.

> Garden Park Paleontology Society
> 330 Royal Gorge Boulevard
> P.O. Box 1957
> Canon City, CO 81215
> (719) 269-7150

Jurupa Mountain Cultural Center

Among its many public programs, the center offers fossil collecting trips. The fossils are all Cenozoic, so no dinosaur material will be found here. Even so, the kids will love it.

> Jurupa Mountain Cultural Center
> 7621 Granite Hill Drive
> Riverside, CA 92509
> (909) 685-5818

Museum of the Rockies

One of the best public paleontology experiences in America, the museum's field program is a real find for aspiring scientists and enthusiastic amateurs. Experts teach courses and lead trips to Montana fossil quarries.

> Museum of the Rockies
> Paleontology Program
> 406 West Kagy Boulevard
> Bozeman, MT 59717
> (406) 994-6618

Old Trail Museum

Great for both adults and children, museum field classes are led by professional paleontologists and may last from a single weekend up to ten days.

> Old Trail Museum
> 523 North Main Street
> Choteau, MT 59422
> (406) 466-5332

Royal Tyrrell Museum of Paleontology

Weekend day digs during warm-weather months allow dino-hunters age sixteen and up to work alongside experts in some of North America's finest dinosaur quarries.

Royal Tyrrell Museum of Paleontology
P.O. Box 7500
Drumheller, Alberta, Canada T0J 0Y0
(888) 440-4240

Timescale Adventures

This nonprofit organization offers hands-on experience in paleontology to the general public. Digs are often conducted on private lands, so finds may be quite unusual if not unique. Research is conducted under the guidance of professional scientists.

Timescale Adventures
P.O. Box 356
Choteau, MT 59422
(800) 238-6873 or (406) 466-5410

University of Wyoming Geology Museum

Field expeditions are offered in cooperation with the Museum of the Rockies at Montana State University. Dino-hunters get to dig for fossils under the guidance of expert paleontologists. Team members must be age fifteen and older. Space is limited, so make arrangements well in advance.

University of Wyoming Geology Museum
P.O. Box 3006
Laramie, WY 82071
(307) 766-2646 (for dinosaur digs)

Wyoming Dinosaur Center and Dig Sites

You can "Dig for a Day" or longer in the quarries near this well-known dinosaur museum. Participants learn firsthand the hard work of field paleontology by helping to excavate, stabilize, and document fossil discoveries.

> Wyoming Dinosaur Center and Dig Sites
> P.O. Box 868
> Thermopolis, WY 82443
> (307) 864-2997 or (800) 455-DINO

Space in the programs described above is often very limited, so be sure to make plans well in advance. You should always call first to find out about schedules, availability, and costs. Be forewarned that some programs—especially those offering lengthy expeditions—can be quite expensive. Fees may run upward of $1,000 or more per individual participant.

9 781581 820355